GROUP C

Sat 14 Jun (5.00pm) Belo Horizonte
COLOMBIA ☐ ☐ GREECE

Sun 15 Jun (2.00am) Recife
IVORY COAST ☐ ☐ JAPAN

Thu 19 Jun (5.00pm) Brasilia
COLOMBIA ☐ ☐ IVORY COAST

Thu 19 Jun (11.00pm) Natal
JAPAN ☐ ☐ GREECE

Tue 24 Jun (9.00pm) Cuiaba
JAPAN ☐ ☐ COLOMBIA

Tue 24 Jun (9.00pm) Fortaleza
GREECE ☐ ☐ IVORY COAST

GROUP D

Sat 14 Jun (8.00pm) Fortaleza
URUGUAY ☐ ☐ COSTA RICA

Sat 14 Jun (11.00pm) Manaus
ENGLAND ☐ ☐ ITALY

Thu 19 Jun (8.00pm) Sao Paulo
URUGUAY ☐ ☐ ENGLAND

Fri 20 Jun (5.00pm) Recife
ITALY ☐ ☐ COSTA RICA

Tue 24 Jun (5.00pm) Natal
ITALY ☐ ☐ URUGUAY

Tue 24 Jun (5.00pm) Belo Horizonte
COSTA RICA ☐ ☐ ENGLAND

GROUP G

Mon 16 Jun (5.00pm) Salvador
GERMANY ☐ ☐ PORTUGAL

Mon 16 Jun (11.00pm) Natal
GHANA ☐ ☐ USA

Sat 21 Jun (8.00pm) Fortaleza
GERMANY ☐ ☐ GHANA

Sun 22 Jun (11.00pm) Manaus
USA ☐ ☐ PORTUGAL

Thu 26 Jun (5.00pm) Recife
USA ☐ ☐ GERMANY

Thu 26 Jun (5.00pm) Brasilia
PORTUGAL ☐ ☐ GHANA

GROUP H

Tue 17 Jun (5.00pm) Belo Horizonte
BELGIUM ☐ ☐ ALGERIA

Tue 17 Jun (11.00pm) Cuiaba
RUSSIA ☐ ☐ SOUTH KOREA

Sun 22 Jun (5.00pm) Rio de Janeiro
BELGIUM ☐ ☐ RUSSIA

Sun 22 Jun (8.00pm) Porto Alegre
SOUTH KOREA ☐ ☐ ALGERIA

Thu 26 Jun (9.00pm) Sao Paulo
SOUTH KOREA ☐ ☐ BELGIUM

Thu 26 Jun (9.00pm) Curitiba
ALGERIA ☐ ☐ RUSSIA

FOR KNOCKOUT STAGES, SEE BACK OF BOOK

THE BIG
BOOK OF THE
WORLD
CUP

BY
CLIVE BATTY AND
JOHN MURRAY

Published by Vision Sports Publishing in 2014

Vision Sports Publishing
19-23 High Street
Kingston upon Thames
Surrey
KT1 1LL

www.visionsp.co.uk

ISBN : 978-1909534-20-9

Editor: Jim Drewett
Authors: Clive Batty and John Murray
Design: Neal Cobourne
Brazil research team: Jill Drewett
Kit images: David Moor, www.historicalkits.co.uk
All pictures: Getty Images

Printed and bound in Slovakia by Neografia

A CIP catalogue record for this book is available from the British Library

All international statistics are correct in *The Big Book of the World Cup*
up until 1 March 2014

CONTENTS

GO NUTS FOR BRAZIL

The waiting is nearly over. Almost exactly three years after Montserrat and Belize played the first game of the lengthy qualification process, the 2014 World Cup will kick off when Brazil play Croatia in Sao Paulo on 12 June. Thirty-two nations, from six continents, playing 64 games, crammed into an action-packed 32-day schedule.

As the most popular sporting event on the planet, the World Cup is always a wonderful occasion, but the 19th edition could be the most special of the lot. Why? Because it is in Brazil.

Brazil defines football as much as football defines Brazil. The country is obsessed with it. Football is played in the parks, on the beaches, in the alleyways – pretty much wherever possible. England might be the home of football but Brazil is the heartbeat of the beautiful game. Not only do Brazilians pride themselves on being the best football-

playing nation – they have won an unprecedented five World Cups – they also do it with style.

Better still, the tournament will be held in the most glorious of settings, with matches played in 12 stadiums all over this picturesque country, famed for its glorious beaches, jaw-dropping landscape and carnival atmosphere. It promises to be a festival of football for those lucky enough to have a ticket or watching the action on the giant screens in the Fan Fests set up in each host city. The Brazilian Tourism Ministry anticipates that a whopping £6.5 billion will be spent by Brazilians and visitors to the country over the four-week period.

The armchair fan is in for a treat too, with the BBC and ITV showing every match live, plus additional highlights packages and coverage online. FIFA estimates that, over the course of the tournament, 26 billion viewers will tune in to the action, and that will of course include a huge chunk of the British population.

England fans at home will be waving their flags and cheering on the team from their sofas (or if things get a bit nervy, from behind their sofas). The Three Lions have been drawn in a tricky group, against four-time winners Italy, reigning Copa America champions Uruguay, and Costa Rica who cruised through CONCACAF qualifying.

The action gets underway for Steven Gerrard, Wayne Rooney and co. against Italy in the sweltering Amazonian city of Manaus on 14 June at 11.00pm, so make sure you don't have to get up early the next day (don't worry, it's a Sunday) before further matches on 19 June (v Uruguay in Sao Paulo, 8.00pm) and 24 June (v Costa Rica in Belo Horizonte, 5.00pm).

While everyone will be hoping England can win their first World Cup since 1966, if things don't go well for Roy Hodgson's men, there are plenty of other reasons to get excited, not least watching the best players and best teams in the world go head to head.

Can Portugal's Cristiano Ronaldo score yet another hat-trick, just as he did to dump Zlatan Ibrahimovic and Sweden out of the World Cup play-offs? Will Argentina's inspiration Lionel Messi run rings around opposition defences, just as he does week in, week out for Barcelona? Could the rampaging Yaya Toure lead Ivory Coast to glory, making them the first African nation to win the World Cup?

All the big nations will be there, including the eight teams who have previously lifted the coveted trophy. In addition to every England match, fixtures you won't want to miss include the rematch of the 2010 final between Spain and the Netherlands, Germany's heavyweight clash against Portugal, and Argentina's showdown with African champions Nigeria.

The Big Guide to the World Cup provides everything the armchair fan needs for the tournament. There's a full match-by-match calendar, so you won't miss a single game, plus a scorechart to keep track of the results. We preview all 32 teams, analysing their chances for the tournament and picking the players to look out for. We have also chosen 11 superstars of Brazil, the best of the best who we expect to make a huge impression in June and July. Which one of these will write their name in history and dominate the World Cup like Pele, Maradona and Zidane have done before them? On top of all that, there's a rundown on the stadiums, features on Brazil, England and the European challenge in South America, plus a detailed records and history section.

Get ready for a month-long football party.

David Luiz and Brazil should provide some hair-raising moments

FOR THE 2014 FIFA WORLD CUP BRAZ

A FEAST OF FOOTBALL

Sixty-four matches over 32 days featuring the best players and best nations on the planet, in the country that created the beautiful game. For armchair fans, the World Cup is footballing nirvana.

The football marathon will run from 12 June when hosts Brazil kick off proceedings against Croatia until the final on 13 July at the Maracana Stadium. Viewers will be treated to up to four live games a day during the group stages, with two daily matches in the knockout phase before the climax of the semi-finals and final.

Better still, there will only be seven days without any football to watch. The full schedule is outlined in our World Cup viewing guide, meaning there is no reason to miss a single game.

The good news for British viewers is that, despite the fact Brazil is more than 5,000 miles away on the other side of the Atlantic, games will be kicking off just as you leave school or finish work for the day. The earliest start time is 5.00pm, with many matches taking place in the middle of the evening and only one game – Ivory Coast

v Japan on 15 June – beginning at 2.00am.

As always, the BBC and ITV will split the live coverage of all the games, with the BBC showing England's opener against Italy on 14 June and ITV broadcasting the Three Lions' two other group matches. The BBC will get first pick of the second-round and semi-final games, while ITV will have priority in the quarter-finals. Both networks will show the final.

And that's not all. As well as a highlights programme on the BBC and ITV each night, and extensive coverage on BBC Radio 5 live, Philip Bernie, BBC head of TV sport, promises this will be "the first truly digital World Cup". All matches will be shown live on both the BBC and ITV websites.

It will be a true football feast in what is shaping up to be a magical month.

WORLD CUP VIEWING GUIDE

All kick-offs are in British Summer Time

GROUP STAGE

THURSDAY 12 JUNE

9.00pm – **Brazil v Croatia**, Sao Paulo, Arena de Sao Paulo (Group A)

FRIDAY 13 JUNE

5.00pm – **Mexico v Cameroon**, Natal, Estadio das Dunas (Group A)

8.00pm – **Spain v Netherlands**, Salvador, Arena Fonte Nova (Group B)

11.00pm – **Chile v Australia**, Cuiaba, Arena Pantanal (Group B)

SATURDAY 14 JUNE

5.00pm – **Colombia v Greece**, Belo Horizonte, Estadio Mineirao (Group C)

8.00pm – **Uruguay v Costa Rica**, Fortaleza, Estadio Castelao (Group D)

11.00pm – **England v Italy**, Manaus, Arena Amazonia (Group D)

SUNDAY 15 JUNE

2.00am – **Ivory Coast v Japan**, Recife, Arena Pernambuco (Group C)

5.00pm – **Switzerland v Ecuador**, Brasilia, Estadio Nacional (Group E)

8.00pm – **France v Honduras**, Porto Alegre, Estadio Beira-Rio (Group E)

11.00pm – **Argentina v Bosnia-Hercegovina**, Rio de Janeiro, Estadio do Maracana (Group F)

MONDAY 16 JUNE

5.00pm – **Germany v Portugal,** Salvador (Group G)

8.00pm – **Iran v Nigeria**, Curitiba, Arena da Baixada (Group F)

11.00pm – **Ghana v USA**, Natal (Group G)

TUESDAY 17 JUNE

5.00pm – **Belgium v Algeria**, Belo Horizonte (Group H)

8.00pm – **Brazil v Mexico**, Fortaleza (Group A)

11.00pm – **Russia v South Korea**, Cuiaba (Group H)

WEDNESDAY 18 JUNE

5.00pm – **Australia v Netherlands**, Porto Alegre (Group B)

8.00pm – **Spain v Chile**, Rio de Janeiro (Group B)

11.00pm – **Cameroon v Croatia**, Manaus (Group A)

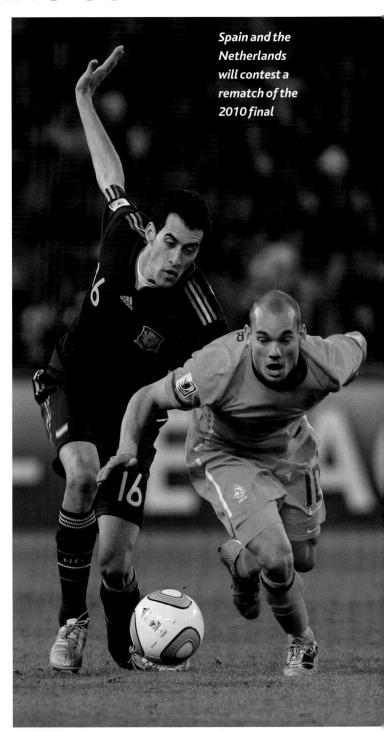

Spain and the Netherlands will contest a rematch of the 2010 final

THURSDAY 19 JUNE

5.00pm – **Colombia v Ivory Coast**, Brasilia (Group C)

8.00pm – **Uruguay v England**, Sao Paulo (Group D)

11.00pm – **Japan v Greece**, Natal (Group C)

FRIDAY 20 JUNE

5.00pm – **Italy v Costa Rica**, Recife (Group D)

8.00pm – **Switzerland v France**, Salvador (Group E)

11.00pm – **Honduras v Ecuador**, Curitiba (Group E)

Match Calendar

SATURDAY 21 JUNE
5.00pm – **Argentina v Iran**, Belo Horizonte (Group F)
8.00pm – **Germany v Ghana**, Fortaleza (Group G)
11.00pm – **Nigeria v Bosnia-Hercegovina**, Cuiaba (Group F)

SUNDAY 22 JUNE
5.00pm – **Belgium v Russia**, Rio de Janeiro (Group H)
8.00pm – **South Korea v Algeria**, Porto Alegre (Group H)
11.00pm – **USA v Portugal**, Manaus (Group G)

Steven Gerrard will hope to lead England through the group stage – and beyond

MONDAY 23 JUNE
5.00pm – **Australia v Spain**, Curitiba (Group B)
5.00pm – **Netherlands v Chile**, Sao Paulo (Group B)
9.00pm – **Cameroon v Brazil**, Brasilia (Group A)
9.00pm – **Croatia v Mexico**, Recife (Group A)

TUESDAY 24 JUNE
5.00pm – **Italy v Uruguay**, Natal (Group D)
5.00pm – **Costa Rica v England**, Belo Horizonte (Group D)
9.00pm – **Japan v Colombia**, Cuiaba (Group C)
9.00pm – **Greece v Ivory Coast**, Fortaleza (Group C)

WEDNESDAY 25 JUNE
5.00pm – **Nigeria v Argentina**, Porto Alegre (Group F)
5.00pm – **Bosnia-Hercegovina v Iran**, Salvador (Group F)
9.00pm – **Honduras v Switzerland**, Manaus (Group E)
9.00pm – **Ecuador v France**, Rio de Janeiro (Group E)

THURSDAY 26 JUNE
5.00pm – **USA v Germany**, Recife (Group G)
5.00pm – **Portugal v Ghana**, Brasilia (Group G)
9.00pm – **South Korea v Belgium**, Sao Paulo (Group H)
9.00pm – **Algeria v Russia**, Curitiba (Group H)

SECOND ROUND

SATURDAY 28 JUNE
1 5.00pm – **Winner Group A v Runner up Group B**, Belo Horizonte
2 9.00pm – **Winner Group C v Runner up Group D**, Rio de Janeiro

SUNDAY 29 JUNE
3 5.00pm – **Winner Group B v Runner up Group A**, Fortaleza
4 9.00pm – **Winner Group D v Runner up Group C**, Recife

MONDAY 30 JUNE
5 5.00pm – **Winner Group E v Runner up Group F**, Brasilia
6 9.00pm – **Winner Group G v Runner up Group H**, Porto Alegre

TUESDAY 1 JULY
7 5.00pm – **Winner Group F v Runner up Group E**, Sao Paulo
8 9.00pm – **Winner Group H v Runner up Group G**, Salvador

QUARTER-FINALS

FRIDAY 4 JULY

QF1 5.00pm – **Winner Match 5 v Winner Match 6**, Rio de Janeiro

QF2 9.00pm – **Winner Match 1 v Winner Match 2**, Fortaleza

SATURDAY 5 JULY

QF3 5.00pm – **Winner Match 7 v Winner Match 8**, Brasilia

QF4 9.00pm – **Winner Match 3 v Winner Match 4**, Salvador

SEMI-FINALS

TUESDAY 8 JULY
9.00pm – **Winner QF1 v Winner QF2**, Belo Horizonte

WEDNESDAY 9 JULY
9.00pm – **Winner QF3 v Winner QF4**, Sao Paulo

3RD/4TH PLACE PLAY-OFF

SATURDAY 12 JULY
9.00pm – Brasilia

WORLD CUP FINAL

SUNDAY 13 JULY
9.00pm – Rio de Janeiro

Will Brazilian strike duo Fred and Neymar be on target on July 13?

A NATION EXPECTS

Football is coming home in 2014. Not to England, the birthplace of the sport, as Three Lions supporters and the FA frequently like to remind us, but to its spiritual home – Brazil.

Think Brazil and you immediately conjure up wondrous images of the rainforest, Copacabana beach, carnival and the magnificent statue of Christ the Redeemer, but most of all you think football. And in Brazil, that means iconic yellow-and-green shirts, romantically named players, mouthwatering ball skills and greats of the game such as Pele, Ronaldo, Garrincha and Socrates.

Brazil is football. Football is Brazil. The two define each other. Brazilians refer to their nation as "o país do futebol" – "the country of football". No other sport comes close. Everyone in Brazil plays or watches football. Everywhere you look, there is football. Every alleyway and street corner has a makeshift goal. The only time

Anyone fancy a quiet kickabout on Ipanema Beach?

those streets are empty is when Brazil are playing. Businesses and banks close for the whole day when Brazil are competing in the World Cup.

Those same businesses and banks might take a month-long holiday this summer when the country welcomes the world to its shores for the tournament it has won more times than anyone else. Sixty-four years after Brazil last hosted the World Cup, it is long overdue. Given how much football, and in particular the World Cup, means to the entire nation, it is certain to be one hell of a party.

Carlos Alberto Torres, captain of the 1970 World Cup-winning team, sums up the importance of football to the Brazilian people. "Football in Brazil is like a religion. Everybody talks about it all the time," he says. "This is the difference between Europe and Brazil. After the World Cup, people in Europe start to think about life, business. Here in Brazil, we breathe football 24 hours a day."

Football arrived in Brazil at the end of the 19th century, first popularised by a group of English ex-pats working on Sao Paulo's railway construction in 1894 at a time when colonial influence remained strong throughout the country. The sport took a few decades to catch on with the masses. Initially, it was played by wealthy clubs in the cities, and only men from upper-class families were accepted onto teams. With Brazil the last country in the Americas to abolish slavery, the black lower classes were shunned by the rest of society. In those early years, the style of play was a far cry from the samba football we know today. Following the English lead, there was a strong emphasis on tactical planning. Teams stuck to rigid formations and played direct football. Little wonder it failed to catch the imagination of the greater public.

But then something changed. Brazil had only become a republic near the end of the 19th century and was still searching for a national identity. Football

provided the answer. It became a game of the people. As doors began to open for black communities and working-class whites in the 1920s, football provided a means for people to express themselves.

Working-class clubs were born and soon competed in the same competitions as the wealthy sides. Black footballers and those of mixed race played a different kind of football – with artistry, flair and moments of individual brilliance – and the country became proud of the players and its heritage. It is no exaggeration to say that the sport unified the nation. From now on, this was the way the game should be played.

Since a lacklustre performance at the first World Cup in 1930, Brazil went from strength to strength to become football's dominant force. The country's successes are well-documented – five World Cup wins, including three of the four tournaments between 1958 and 1970, plus the player commonly heralded as the best to have kicked a ball, Pele.

Upon awarding the 2014 World Cup to Brazil in 2007, FIFA president Sepp Blatter paid tribute to the country's standing in the game. "This is the country that has given to the world the best football and the best footballers, and they are five-times world champions," he said.

Brazilians are understandably proud of their achievements and the fact that their country is the only one to have played in every World Cup. Anything other than victory on home soil will be seen as a failure, as Brazil coach Luiz Felipe Scolari – who is hoping to repeat his success from Korea and Japan in 2002 – explains.

"The players know they will have to win the World Cup. We can't play a tournament in Brazil and think that second place will do," Scolari says.

If Scolari's words sound over-dramatic, then it is worth revisiting the last time Brazil hosted the tournament in 1950. A year that still strikes fear into the entire nation.

There was no World Cup final in 1950, but instead a four-team round-robin of the group winners from the first stage. After scoring 13 goals and conceding just two in

There are good Brazilian players, there are great Brazilian players, and then there's Pele

their first two matches, the hosts were overwhelming favourites to win the tournament, requiring only a draw against Uruguay in their final game in front of 199,854 at the Maracana Stadium (football's highest ever recorded attendance). Despite taking the lead, Brazil conceded two goals in the second half to achieve the unthinkable: losing a World Cup on home soil.

A national crisis unfolded. Many suicides were reported, including two spectators at the game who jumped from the stands of the Maracana. The country felt ashamed. Several newspapers did not acknowledge the result, while a renowned radio journalist was so dismayed that he retired. From that day on, Brazil refused to wear their 'cursed' all white; thus the famous yellow-and-green strip was born.

"There are many people in Brazil who are haunted by the memory of what happened the last time we hosted, in 1950," Jorginho, a member of Brazil's victorious 1994 World Cup side, says. "We reached the final match, only to be beaten by Uruguay: a day of national mourning."

Several players retired in the aftermath, while others were never selected for their country again. But no one suffered more than Moacir Barbosa. The Brazilian

goalkeeper, who was at fault for the winning goal, remained a scapegoat for the rest of his days, not even allowed to meet the players in the build-up to the 1994 World Cup for fear of jinxing them. He revealed that the worst moment of his life came many years later when he overheard a woman say to her son at a market: "Look at him, son. He is the man that made all of Brazil cry."

Despite the country's many triumphs since 1950, the Uruguay loss continues to torture Brazil and casts a shadow over this summer. Every time a World Cup comes around, there is always pressure on Brazil to win the tournament. But the 2014 World Cup will be on a different scale.

The whole country is desperate to avoid a repeat of those catastrophic events from 1950, but will the overwhelming pressure, the demand to banish the ghost from 64 years ago, prove too much for Scolari and his 23-man squad? Given that 1950 remains fresh in everyone's minds and the added burdens that playing on home soil will bring, with every move to be scrutinised by the media and public alike, it will be quite some feat if Brazil live up to their tag as trophy favourites and walk away with the cup on 13 July.

The goal that haunts a nation: Moacir Barbosa's mistake gifts Uruguay the 1950 World Cup

The iconic Maracana Stadium will host the 2014 World Cup final – will Brazil be in it?

Zico jostles with Claudio Gentile in the classic match against Italy in 1982

Making the coach's task even harder is the reality that merely winning the tournament will not be sufficient; it must be won with style. To Brazilians, football means a whole lot more than a game between two teams trying to kick the ball into the opposition's net. There are certain requirements – a philosophy – that their players must meet whenever they step onto the field. Yes, they should win, but they also must play with creativity, rhythm and swagger, showing individual skill and genius to create collective harmony, and expressing joy when they do so. "Joga bonito," the fans cry. The translation? "Play beautifully."

There was nothing more beautiful than Carlos Alberto's famous goal in the 1970 World Cup final, his right-foot piledriver the finishing touch to a nine-player move that involved some of the great names of Brazilian football.

Style and aesthetics are almost as important as the result. A case in point is the Brazilian national team of 1982. Much like Hungary in 1954 and the Netherlands in 1974, this side is remembered more than the country that won the tournament and, in its home nation, more fondly than the less expressive teams of 1994 and 2002 that actually lifted the trophy.

Falcao, Socrates and Zico are held in just as high acclaim as Ronaldinho or Romario. Playing four attacking midfielders, they mesmerised the football world in Spain that summer with their devastating play, and the heartbreaking 3-2 loss to Italy that ensured their elimination – however naïve it may have been – only heightened their appeal.

That unforgettable game in 1982, often hailed as the best in World Cup history, was described by Zico as the day football died. It was a triumph for the system – a typically cautious and resistant Italian approach – over the individuals.

Such was the emphasis on attack in the Brazil teams of years gone by that there was a common perception they didn't know how to defend; scoring more goals than the opposition was all that mattered. But since 1982, while they continue to show moments of individual flamboyance, they have been forced to adapt the way they play, to something closer to the stronger, more robotic, pressing style of the Europeans.

The 1994 and 2002 World Cup-winning teams are evidence of this, both far more functional and hard-working than previous Brazil teams. When you consider that in one UEFA Champions League week during the

David Luiz would love to swap the Confederations Cup for another trophy this summer

group stage in 2013, 32 Brazilian players were in the starting line-ups (as opposed to only seven Englishmen, but that's another story), it's hardly surprising there has been such an overwhelming European influence on the national team.

A key reason why so many players leave behind their homeland is to put their talent on show in Europe and win a call-up for their country. You won't see any of the club v country rows that erupt almost on a monthly basis between the Premier League sides and English national team. Playing for Brazil is the number one goal.

There is also the lure of financial gains in a country where large parts are wrought with poverty. To many, professional football is a way to a different life, a way out from the destitution of the favelas, a means to providing for your family. There are no shortage of top players who took the journey from the slums to stardom. Pele famously grew up using a stuffed sock or grapefruit as a ball, while 2002 World Cup captain Cafu and one of the stars of that tournament, Rivaldo, both came from favelas.

Whatever their background, you can guarantee that the whole of Brazil will be glued to the action when their team kicks off the tournament against Croatia on 12 June. The 12 host cities will each have a Fan Fest location, an area where fans not lucky enough to have a ticket can gather to watch the games on giant screens. First trialled at the Germany World Cup in 2006, the Fan Fests have proved spectacularly popular with millions of supporters, of all nationalities, and will be based in iconic locations all over Brazil. None more so than Copacabana Beach in Rio de Janeiro. Three million people gathered there in July 2013 for the final mass of the Pope's visit to Brazil. Expect similar scenes this summer.

The atmosphere will be something to savour up and down the country. For a nation famed for its carnival, it is certain to be a spectacular party, whatever happens. Should Brazil go all the way to glory, the celebrations will be on a different scale altogether.

The centerpiece of it all will be the Maracana. Now with a reduced capacity but even more majestic, the rejuvenated stadium will host the World Cup's final match, as in 1950. For a nation that eats, breathes and sleeps football, there would be no better place for Brazil to lift a sixth World Cup. Redemption for the horrors of 64 years past. Unadulterated joy for the country that created the beautiful game.

A World Cup in Brazil is guaranteed to have a carnival atmosphere

Top left: A Papal visit in 2013 attracted three million people on Copacabana Beach. Brazil fans show their support in many ways – wearing the colours with pride (top right), flag-waving (right) ... and impersonating a Christmas tree (above)

England will need lion-hearted performances from Daniel Sturridge, Wayne Rooney and Steven Gerrard

NO PRESSURE ON ENGLAND

Something feels different this time. For the first time in many years, England are going to a World Cup without the whole country demanding success. Free from the choking expectation of everyone predicting they will bring the trophy home, could Roy Hodgson's Three Lions thrive in a pressure-free environment and spring a surprise in Brazil?

In World Cups gone by, the Three Lions have entered the tournament with genuine expectations, a demand even, from the public, press and bookmakers alike, of lifting the trophy for the first time since 1966.

Not now.

With the failures of Germany and South Africa still fresh in everyone's minds, there were no over-the-top celebrations when Steven Gerrard sealed England's spot in Brazil with the second goal in the final qualifier against Poland, but instead recognition of a job well done and acknowledgement of a tough road ahead. Yes, we're all excited, but let's not get too carried away (for the time being at least).

That feeling continued after the draw for the finals was made. The bookies installed England at a best price of 33/1 to bring the trophy home, meaning they were not even among the top 10 most fancied teams. Again, a fair assessment – after all, that reflected their position in the FIFA rankings (13th at time of publication) and the fact that they were drawn in a nasty-looking group, with Euro 2012 finalists Italy, 2010 World Cup semi-finalists Uruguay, and a dangerous Costa Rica side.

Keeping everyone's feet on the ground has been a constant theme of Roy Hodgson's reign as England manager, as he showed in his reaction to the draw. Here was a man who just wanted to get on with his job. "It does not surprise me at all to get a tough draw. But I am still very positive about the whole affair, as you never know," he said.

"The only prediction I'm going to make is that there will be three cracking games. There will be plenty of speculation. I will get on trying to prepare the team."

Since replacing Fabio Capello in early 2012, Hodgson has done a solid, if unspectacular job. With little time to prepare for Euro 2012, England always seemed unlikely to be genuine challengers, particularly with star striker Wayne Rooney sitting out the first two games through suspension. And so it proved as they did well to top their group before being shown up by Italy in the quarter-finals, eventually bowing out in the traditional manner of a penalty shoot-out defeat. A school report might have given them a 'B minus'. Decent effort but could do better.

Hodgson then successfully steered the Three Lions through their World Cup qualifying campaign. It was never easy, and there were a couple of scares along the way but, at the end of it, England's record was six wins and four draws from their 10 games, with 31 goals scored and just four conceded. Going into this summer, it is worth remembering that England remain unbeaten

England manager Roy Hodgson has blended a team of youth and experience

in competitive games under Hodgson.

That's not to say Hodgson has been without criticism (he wouldn't be an England manager if he hadn't, right?). His team has shown some flaws which every Three Lions fan knows all too well – can't keep hold of the ball, lack creativity, throw away a one-goal lead. There have been some friendly internationals where England have been shown up by slicker, more technically gifted sides, with the back-to-back Wembley defeats to Chile and Germany springing to mind.

But through it all, there remains a positive feeling that this is an England team on the rise. Hodgson deserves praise for juggling the demands of qualification with introducing fresh blood to the side. The selection of young Tottenham winger Andros Townsend for the crunch games against Montenegro

Tottenham winger Andros Townsend just loves playing for his country

and Poland was a perfect example, with the debutant delivering two man-of-the match performances.

The manager has seamlessly blended new talent with old heads, keeping some experience in the side without completely wiping out the golden generation. Gerrard remains as captain, with Rooney the talisman up front, but around them there are plenty of fresh faces.

Take the defence, for example. Throughout qualifying, there wasn't a Rio Ferdinand or John Terry in sight, as Phil Jagielka and Gary Cahill built a partnership in central defence, with Manchester United youngsters Phil Jones and Chris Smalling on standby. Glen Johnson faces stiff competition from Kyle Walker at right-back, while Leighton Baines seems to have leapfrogged Ashley Cole on the left. Behind them, Joe Hart remains the firm choice as goalkeeper and should stay there for years to come.

"It has been a collective effort over two years," Gerrard said after qualification was secured. "The manager has created a great blend of youth and experience.

"We have proved there is hope. There is big confidence within the group. It is important to stay

humble, as there is a long way to go."

Tactically too, Hodgson has shown progression. After mixed results with his dated 4-4-2 formation, England now line up in a 4-2-3-1. As with every tournament, injuries often dictate who will be in the starting line-up, but if everyone has a clean bill of health, Arsenal's Jack Wilshere or maybe even Everton teenager Ross Barkley are best placed to keep Gerrard company in the middle of the park.

The lone striker – likely to be Daniel Sturridge – plays in front of Rooney and two pacey widemen. While the loss of Theo Walcott to a serious knee injury is a blow, Hodgson has no shortage of options to choose from, with Townsend, his Spurs compatriot Aaron Lennon, Manchester United duo Danny Welbeck and Ashley Young, Liverpool teenager Raheem Sterling and Southampton captain Adam Lallana just some of the names in contention. The days of Rooney starting up front alongside Emile Heskey seem a long time ago.

The formation and supporting cast might be different, but Rooney remains the star performer. England's one player of genuine world class, Rooney has once again performed to the very highest heights for Manchester United in 2013/14, while so many of his team-mates have slumped in form, and he thrived for the Three Lions in qualification. However, it is no secret that the World Cup remains a blot on his copybook, a combination of injury, poor form and lack of discipline meaning he is yet to shine on the biggest stage of all.

England's captain and coach are in no doubt how important Rooney is to the team's chances in Brazil. "It would make a massive difference if Wayne can do well at the finals. It will be the difference between us going home early or staying in the tournament a long time," Gerrard revealed.

"Everyone who does well at World Cups has a scorer who gets four or five goals and Wayne is the man capable of producing for us.

"Wayne is in tremendous form and if we are to go to a World Cup, surprise a few and do well, then we need him fired up. If you have Wayne Rooney firing and scoring goals, you have a better chance."

Hodgson backed up his captain: "If the question is: 'Do I believe Wayne Rooney has got the ability to be a star at this tournament?' Then the answer is: 'Yes, of course'."

England will be relying on a stellar performance from Rooney and several others if they are to make their way out of one of the trickiest groups. It doesn't

come any tougher than their opening two matches against Italy and Uruguay, who boast six World Cup successes between them. When you add the factors of playing in another continent, with a different climate and conditions – including the humid hotbed of Manaus in the Amazon for their first match – and the large travelling distances involved, their task looks even harder.

If they survive the group stage, the Three Lions' draw will get slightly kinder, on paper at any rate, with Colombia or Ivory Coast the likely opponents. After that, though, Brazil, Spain or the Netherlands will probably be waiting in the quarter-finals. Get that far, and the lid of expectation will be well and truly blown off, no matter what anyone says.

While we shouldn't get too far ahead of ourselves, there's no harm in looking wistfully at an omen from half a century ago. The last time England played Uruguay in a competitive match was in the group stage of the 1966 World Cup. And we all know what happened after that.

Top: Wayne Rooney will carry the nation's hopes on his shoulders. Right: Can Daniel Sturridge replicate his scoring form for Liverpool in an England shirt?

Steven Gerrard does his best plane celebration after scoring the goal that booked England's flight to Brazil

The opposition

With two former World Cup champions and the underrated Costa Rica in their group, England face a tough test to progress to the knockout phase.

England v Italy, Manaus
Saturday 14 June
11.00pm, BBC

It wasn't the welcome the Three Lions were hoping for. When the draw was made for the 2014 World Cup, pairing England and Italy in Manaus for their opening Group D encounter, the Mayor of the Amazonian city said: "We would prefer that England doesn't come. We hope to get a better team and a coach who is more sensible and polite. [Roy Hodgson] is one of the few people in the world who is not curious about the Amazon, who doesn't want to know about Manaus."

The comments were in response to what the England boss had said a few days earlier, citing his concerns about the city's "problematic" climate, with its tropical nature unlikely to suit the northern European teams.

While Hodgson quickly played down his comments after the draw, it's easy to see why he was worried. The conditions will be far from ideal in a roasting Manaus with temperatures above 30 degrees and humidity levels up to 90 per cent. The second-half performances in Japan during the 2002 World Cup are an all too recent reminder of England's tendency to wilt in the heat.

Perhaps most telling of all was the reaction of Tottenham's Brazilian midfielder Sandro to England's match at the Arena Amazonia. "It is a big city, but it is so deep in the Amazon. Most Brazilians haven't been there," he said. "I want to go there. To fish, though, not to play football."

Luckily for England, their opponents Italy will be facing exactly the same challenges, although the southern Europeans may be better equipped to cope with the heat. If the Three Lions are to get off to a winning start, they will have to create history in the process, having never previously beaten Italy at a major tournament.

Nevertheless, the traditionally cautious Italians are slow out of the blocks at the start of the tournament, putting an emphasis on not losing. Since the 1982 World Cup, they have won just three of their eight opening matches, drawing four times and famously losing to the Republic of Ireland in 1994.

After limping out of the 2010 World Cup bottom of their group, the four-time champions have been revitalised under coach Cesare Prandelli, reaching the final of Euro 2012 and going through World Cup qualification undefeated. Hodgson will be well aware of the threats posed by the likes of livewire forward Mario Balotelli and midfield general Andrea Pirlo after England were knocked out of Euro 2012 by the Italians in the quarter-finals. Italy won on penalties, but it was remarkable that the match lasted so long, such was their dominance over 120 minutes.

Deep in the furnace of the Amazon, England will need significant improvement if they are to avoid becoming hot under the collar once again.

Andrea Pirlo (left) got the better of Wayne Rooney and England in the Euro 2012 quarter-finals

Uruguay v England, Sao Paulo
Thursday 19 June
8.00pm, ITV

England will relish being back in the more familiar surroundings of a cooler Sao Paulo for their second match, with temperatures unlikely to rise above 20 degrees and a 30 per cent chance of rain.

However, the Three Lions' task will not get any easier on the field against Uruguay, the reigning Copa America champions, who reached the last four in South Africa. Now in the comfort of their own continent, the two-time previous winners should pose a formidable threat.

The Uruguayans boast a frontline that will make defences across the globe tremble. Liverpool's deadly frontman Luis Suarez will pair up with Paris Saint-Germain hotshot Edinson Cavani, with the option of changing the formation to a 4-3-3 to include veteran striker Diego Forlan, winner of the Golden Ball in South Africa. Suarez, in particular, will strike fear into the English defenders, who have seen his skills at first-hand in the Premier League on a regular basis.

Nevertheless, for all Uruguay's attacking prowess, England should take heart from the fact that they are

England must keep Edinson Cavani and Luis Suarez quiet

shaky at the back, shipping 25 goals in 16 qualifying games, and the ageing team only reached Brazil after overcoming Jordan in a play-off.

Just as with Italy, the Three Lions have never got the better of Uruguay at a World Cup, but if they can find a way to stop Suarez, the battle will be half won.

Costa Rica v England, Belo Horizonte
Thursday 24 June
5.00pm, ITV

Pitted in a group with three nations that boast seven World Cup wins between them, Costa Rica have unsurprisingly been cast in the role of rank outsiders. However, they shouldn't be written off too easily, having qualified comfortably for Brazil behind CONCACAF winners, the United States.

If England are to get out of Group D, it is likely that they will need to win this match at the Estadio Mineirao in Belo Horizonte. While conditions won't be as stifling as the Amazon, it will still be dry and warm with temperatures expected to hit 25 degrees.

The Three Lions have never played Costa Rica before but should not take their opponents lightly or they may suffer the same fate as Scotland back in 1990. The Scots infamously lost 1-0 to Costa Rica in the group stage of Italia '90, a result which ultimately ensured that Los Ticos progressed at their expense.

English fans will be familiar with the Costa Rican

captain, Fulham's Bryan Ruiz, now on loan at PSV Eindhoven, while Arsenal striker Joel Campbell – on loan at Olympiakos – is another key figure. If Ruiz's comments in the aftermath of the draw are anything to go by, then his country holds no fear.

"We want to leverage the positive part and confront three teams that have made history worldwide. The draw was beautiful and a surprise. It was a nice opportunity," he said. "We have to play three perfect games and that's what we will prepare for."

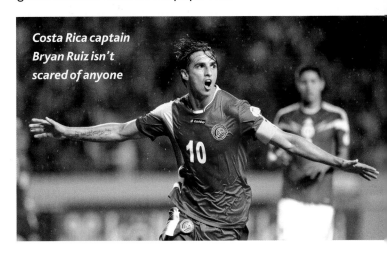

Costa Rica captain Bryan Ruiz isn't scared of anyone

Home from home

England have picked Rio de Janeiro as their base for the World Cup and will train in the shadows of Sugar Loaf Mountain.

Will staying at the Royal Tulip Hotel help England blossom?

First there was the circus of Baden-Baden, with the shopaholic WAGs attracting the attention of the world's press in the German spa resort. Four years later came the other extreme, the boredom of Rustenburg, where the England players' enforced idleness was matched by a lack of inspiration on the pitch.

In 2014, the FA appear to have learned from past mistakes and have opted for the middle ground when it comes to choosing a base camp during the World Cup. Roy Hodgson and his 23-man squad will be based in the Royal Tulip Hotel in the Barra district of Rio de Janeiro.

After the debacle of 2010, David Bernstein, chairman of the FA at the time, vowed that England would be "good tourists" in the future, and the choice of Rio continues the theme established at Euro 2012 when the team stayed in the centre of the popular Polish city, Krakow, and were often seen out and about.

Overlooking Sao Conrado Beach, the five-star Royal Tulip Hotel has recently been refurbished, has a giant swimming pool and is ideally located next to the Gavea Golf Course and an upmarket mall. The team will train at the nearby Urca military base, in the shadows of Sugarloaf Mountain.

Much like the World Cup itself, choosing the right base is a highly competitive business between the 32 teams and England wasted no time in picking their hotel. "We have made plans already, we have discussed where we are going to stay with FIFA," Alex Horne, the FA's general secretary, said after qualification was confirmed. "You have to be ahead of the game on this."

While none of England's group games will be in Rio, they only face one lengthy plane journey – the 1,771-mile trip to Manaus for their match against Italy – with the other matches in Sao Paulo (223 miles) and Belo Horizonte (226 miles).

"Our great advantage will be being based in Rio, as we will only have one long trip," Hodgson said. "If we'd had three games up in the north, it would have been difficult."

The FA have done everything possible to aid England's cause. They scheduled a friendly in late May at Wembley against another South American opponent, Peru, with the Uruguay match in mind, then England will go to a training camp in Miami, which should replicate the heat and humidity of the Amazon, where they will play warm-up matches against Honduras and Ecuador. After that, it will be time to set up camp in Rio.

"We've already decided that we'll go with the team [to Manaus] two days before, not the usual one day before, and we hope that acclimatisation and the acclimatisation in Miami before will stand us in good stead," Hodgson revealed.

If England get through their group, their second-round match will either be a stone's throw away from their base at the Maracana or 1,165 miles north in Recife. On the plus side, Recife is very wet in June and July so would feel just like home. That is the aim after all.

United we fall

When the USA played England at the 1950 World Cup in Brazil, the result made headlines around the sporting world.

It was the result that no one saw coming. The unloseable game. The shock to beat all sporting shocks.

USA 1 England 0. Or to put it another way, Ragtag bunch of amateurs and semi-professionals 1 Country that invented football 0. Roy Hodgson and his squad may face a challenging draw in Brazil this summer, but surely they will avoid the shame heaped upon their predecessors the last time the World Cup was held in the country. Quite simply, England's loss to the USA in 1950 stands alongside North Korea's win over Italy in 1966 and Cameroon's upstaging of reigning champions Argentina in 1990 as the greatest upset in World Cup history.

When England arrived in Brazil 64 years ago, expectations were at an all-time high. Remarkably, it was the first time the country that created the sport had entered a World Cup, due to squabbles with FIFA and deeming the tournament between the home nations to be of greater importance. The word from Walter Winterbottom's squad in Brazil was that, now they had bothered to show up, they expected to take the trophy home at the first time of asking. And with players of the quality of the evergreen Stanley Matthews, flying winger Tom Finney and captain Billy Wright, that seemed a reasonable assumption.

Things started well enough, thanks to a routine 2-0 win over Chile at the Maracana, while the USA slumped to a 3-1 loss to Spain. With England's second match against the American part-timers in Belo Horizonte, qualification for the next stage seemed assured.

Even the USA's coach, Bill Jeffrey, sensed a lost cause, telling the press before the game that his team had "no chance". After all, the side was cobbled together from all sorts of nationalities, including a Scottish winger and Belgian left-back. Some of their players hadn't made the trip to Brazil due to not getting time off work; one who had was a postman, while another – goalkeeper Frank Borghi – drove a hearse.

Aptly enough, in the match itself, Borghi played a pivotal role in delivering the last rights to England, pulling off a series of saves to deny wave after wave of

Tom Finney wins a header between two Americans – about the only thing England won all day!

attack. But the man who grabbed the headlines was a Haitian, Joe Gaetjens, deflecting a shot past England keeper Bert Williams seven minutes before half-time to score the game's only goal. The inevitable English barrage followed, but a combination of the woodwork (five times), fluffed opportunities and Borghi's heroics kept them out.

Some newspapers printed the result as 10-1 to England, assuming the original wired report was a typing error. The players were equally shell-shocked, crashing out of the tournament after defeat in their next game to Spain before making a hasty retreat home. The royal blue shirts which the team wore that day were quickly abandoned, but the infamous result in Belo Horizonte will never be scrubbed from the record.

England will be hoping history does not repeat itself when they return to the city for their group match against Costa Rica.

THE FINAL FRONTIER

It is European football's equivalent of breaking into Fort Knox. The impossible challenge or, as it's otherwise known, winning the World Cup on South American soil.

Four times in the history of football's greatest competition, the best teams from Europe have travelled west to take on the might of South America and the rest of the world. Four times they have come away empty-handed, often with their collective tails between their legs. If you throw Central America and the similar climate conditions of the Mexico tournaments of 1970 and 1986 into the mix, it takes the total to a miserable six failures from six attempts.

Between them, the 13 European qualifiers for Brazil 2014 have won 10 World Cups and have been on the losing side in the final another 10 times. Their countries can boast many of the world's best players, who play

week in week out in the most formidable domestic leagues as well as the highest-quality competition of the lot, the UEFA Champions League. European nations have won the past two World Cups and, since 1990, Brazil are the only side from another continent to have tasted global glory.

But when it comes to South America, it is a whole different ball game. Uruguay 1930, Brazil 1950, Chile 1962 or Argentina 1978 – different host nations but each time the same result. A World Cup victory for a South American country.

The Dutch are dejected after falling short in the 1978 World Cup final

Now, in June, Europe's finest will arrive in Brazil, aiming to live up to their reputation as the world's footballing powerhouse and put right this wrong once and for all. Can they prove the South American curse is nothing more than a statistical anomaly or will they follow in the footsteps of Platini, Charlton, Rossi and so many other luminaries before them and come away empty-handed?

If you listen to some of the leading figures in world football, it feels like they might as well stay at home. Former Germany striker Karl-Heinz Rummenigge, who played in the Argentina World Cup in 1978 as well as the final in 1982 and 1986, believes it will be another tale of European woe.

"I fear it won't be different this time," he said. "A country from South America like Brazil or Argentina will become world champions. They will try to compensate for the loss at the last two World Cups."

Meanwhile, his countryman Oliver Bierhoff, part of Joachim Low's managerial team for the German national side, reckons a European win will be "almost impossible". "It is a really big mountain," he said. "The South American sides are usually more advanced."

And we haven't got started on England yet, where the picture is even more bleak for England according to former national boss Glenn Hoddle. "It is unrealistic for England to think they can go and win the World Cup in Brazil," he said. "Spain have Europe's best chance, but even then they probably only have a 35 per cent chance. England have got a lesser chance than that. I don't want to put a percentage on that."

Making the task considerably harder for the 13 European teams is the current strength of the South American nations. Four years ago, all five South American teams reached the knockout stage, with only Chile failing to make the quarter-finals. On home soil, the indications are that they will most likely improve on that performance.

At the end of the 2014 World Cup qualifying period, South America had three teams in the top six of the FIFA World Rankings – Argentina (third), Colombia (fourth) and Uruguay (sixth). And that didn't even include Brazil, the host nation, five-time world champions and many people's favourites for the tournament, who were 11th. Chile, meanwhile, fresh from a classy 2-0 defeat of England at Wembley, were 12th. Such is the continent's prowess that, of the six South American teams to have qualified for Brazil, only Ecuador (22nd) seem without a realistic chance of going deep into the tournament.

Spain's David Villa celebrates the first win for a European country outside its continent in 2010

Nor should we forget the other 13 nations from around the world who will be taking part. There have been many outstanding performances from other continents – Cameroon in 1990 and South Korea in 2002 immediately spring to mind – often at the expense of a traditional European force. Pele's prediction that an African side would win the World Cup by 2000 continues to haunt him, but the likes of Ivory Coast and Nigeria should be a tough match for anyone, with England manager Roy Hodgson talking up their chances.

"I think they [African nations] may have a stronger chance than any of the European teams, to be perfectly honest, because of the climate," Hodgson said. "There are many African players out there of excellent quality now. They play in the top European leagues and that makes the African nations very strong."

Luiz Suarez and Uruguay could be a major threat

Hodgson may ultimately be proved right, but given that the African teams didn't come close to winning the World Cup – or, Ghana aside, even getting out of their group – in South Africa, the chances of them doing so further afield appear slim. The simple truth is that it is harder to win the World Cup outside your time (or comfort) zone.

Forget South America for a moment; of the 10 World Cups to be held in Europe, only one has been won by a non-European nation. And that was the Brazil side at the 1958 World Cup in Sweden, blessed with the likes of Garrincha, Vava and a 17-year-old Pele, who were just starting out on a run that would bring an unprecedented three World Cup triumphs in 12 years.

Thirteen of the 19 World Cups have been won by a nation from the host continent (15 if you push the boundaries slightly and include the two Mexico tournaments). As the host nation, you have an even greater chance of success – six times the country which has staged the tournament has gone on to lift the trophy in front of its own fans.

To be fair to the South Americans, while they may have failed to take Europe by storm, they have prospered elsewhere with the Brazilians coming out on top in Sweden (1958), the USA (1994) and Korea/Japan (2002), as well as Mexico in 1970 where Argentina also emerged victorious 16 years later. On the other hand, Spain's victory in the 2010 World Cup in South Africa was notable not only for being the country's first global title, but also the first time any European team had got their hands on the trophy outside of their own continent.

And it is Spain that could hold the key to unlocking the South American safe. The reigning world champions have recorded victories in all corners of the globe since they kicked off their trophy-winning odyssey at Euro 2008. According to former England and Southampton star Matthew Le Tissier, the Spanish style of play will be pivotal to their hopes this summer.

"Spain are Europe's top contenders because they expend less energy the way they play," he said. "Their

style is more suited to South American football. They move the ball about so well they have got their passing and movement down to an art form almost.

"Their passing in midfield opens teams up and it's hard to get the ball back when you are playing them. But being such an offensive team they are always susceptible to the counter-attack when they leave gaps at the back."

While adopting the South American style of play may not be a viable solution for all the European teams, particularly an England side schooled on the hustle and bustle of the Premier League, one factor that won't be such a disadvantage this time is travel.

The four European teams who participated in 1930 only had one option to get to Uruguay: by boat. A three-week trip was hardly the ideal preparation for competing in a World Cup, especially when it came to maintaining player fitness, and many countries refused to play for precisely that reason.

While air travel was in use by the time the tournament was held in Brazil in 1950, flying was

a completely different experience to what we know today, and that also applied at Chile 1962 and, to a lesser extent, Argentina 1978. And for all these tournaments, it wasn't just getting to the country that was a problem; it was getting around once you were there as well, with teams required to travel long distances in less than ideal conditions.

There are no such problems today, of course. Elite footballers are used to travelling from country to country, with top-level support teams making their journey as comfortable as possible. While the nations will be building up some significant mileage around Brazil, it won't be any different from the distances travelled in Poland and Ukraine at Euro 2012, or South Africa two years before that. And every journey will be planned meticulously.

Advances in technology may help the Europeans get over their travel sickness but, as every English cricketer knows, there's not much you can do about the weather.

Sergio Aguero is one of several star strikers for Argentina

England wilted in the heat of Japan against Brazil in the 2002 World Cup quarter-finals

Brazil will be hot and humid, not conditions that European teams tend to thrive in, as England will testify from their energy-sapping experiences in the second halves of games at Korea/Japan 2002.

The trend of modern football is that all the best South Americans players move to Europe, to compete in the holy grail that is the Champions League, not the other way around. As such, European players have very little experience of playing in such conditions, a factor which Roy Hodgson believes may be critical.

"Even in winter months we are seeing 33 degrees [in Brazil]. We don't play any games at 33 degrees heat and humidity in England," he said.

The England manager also cites the playing surface as another potential problem area.

"Second, the grass is different. There is nowhere near as much pace on the ball as you get in Europe. So teams will find that a little bit difficult.

"Also the pitches are very wide, certainly as wide as any we have got in England or even wider. And the South Americans have got all these unbelievably technical players."

Perhaps Hodgson's last sentence is the most important of the lot. There is no doubt that the European challenge in years gone by has been hindered by travel and unfamiliar conditions, while their South American counterparts have made the most of home comforts. However, if you don't have quality technical players – a common lament in England – ultimately you're not going to win the tournament.

If the likes of Spain, Germany, Italy and the Netherlands can adapt to the conditions to recreate their formidable game plans, then they have every chance of success. It is also worth remembering that, despite all the variables and meticulous preparations, the winning team will rely on one other crucial factor. But this is something that cannot be controlled, whichever continent they are from – a healthy slice of luck.

Continental rift

While European nations have lifted the World Cup 10 times, tournaments in South America have not proved a happy hunting ground.

URUGUAY 1930

Four months before the inaugural World Cup kicked off, the chances of a European nation entering, let alone winning, the tournament appeared slim, with no side from the continent registering as a participant before the February deadline. England and the other home nations were not welcome, having withdrawn from FIFA in the wake of an argument over payments to amateurs, while other leading countries refused to take part in a competition which they believed should be held in Europe.

Ultimately, four nations – Belgium, France, Romania and Yugoslavia – made the gruelling trip to Uruguay by

The Uruguayan team of 1930 dominated the World Cup on their own turf

boat to compete in the 13-team event. They must have wished they'd stayed at home. Only the Yugoslavians advanced from their group, with the other three teams managing just two wins between them.

Once in the semi-finals, Yugoslavia were on the wrong end of a 6-1 drubbing by eventual winners Uruguay. Argentina inflicted the same scoreline on the USA – who had several Englishmen in their ranks – to ensure an all-South American final. For Europe, the first World Cup was a costly and humbling experience.

BRAZIL 1950

With much of Europe still reeling from the devastating effects of World War II, the tournament returned to South America in 1950. Twenty years on from the inaugural competition, the story was much the same. Uruguay lifted the trophy once again, beating South American rivals Brazil in the decider and throwing the host nation into mourning in the process.

This time, England turned up, amid plenty of fanfare after resolving their disagreement with FIFA four years earlier. Their pre-tournament boasts quickly came back to bite them when they lost a group match to the USA in what remains one of the greatest World Cup shocks

Zito leaps for joy after scoring Brazil's second goal against Czechoslovakia in the 1962 final

(see page 29). That result meant an early exit for the English, alongside fellow Europeans Italy, Switzerland and Yugoslavia who also failed to get out of their groups.

Spain and Sweden enjoyed better fortunes, however, progressing to the final round-robin of four teams. But that was as good as it got, as neither side was a match for Uruguay or Brazil, with the latter putting a combined 13 goals past the Europeans.

CHILE 1962

The 1962 showpiece had a strong European flavour with no fewer than 10 nations taking part. Given that there were only 16 teams in the whole tournament, the chances of European success were stacked in their favour, particularly after six sides from the continent qualified for the quarter-finals.

That total included England who were quickly learning what was required at the global tournament and advanced from their group at the expense of Argentina. In the last eight they were unlucky to run into an exceptional Brazil side, succumbing 3-1.

The sole other South American survivor, Chile, also reached the semi-finals thanks to a 2-1 win against the Soviet Union, before the host nation fell to the rampant Brazilians. In the other semi-final, Czechoslovakia edged past Yugoslavia to make a small slice of history as the first Europeans to reach a final in South America.

There was no shame in losing to Brazil in the final but that result, coupled with Chile's third-place victory over Yugoslavia, reinforced the aura of South American dominance, however outnumbered they might have been.

ARGENTINA 1978

England may have failed to qualify for their second World Cup in succession, but once again Europe had a strong representation with 10 teams on show. None more talented than the Netherlands who had missed out in the final four years earlier.

Humiliated by Peru and then held by Iran in their opening two matches, Scotland were one of five European teams who failed to advance to the second group stage, a rousing 3-2 win against the Dutch being too little, too late. With the format dictating that the group winner in the second phase would qualify for the final, the Netherlands rediscovered their form to edge out Italy and West Germany, while in the battle of the South Americans, Argentina squeezed past Brazil on goal difference, courtesy of a controversial 6-0 demolition of the hapless Peruvians.

The host nation, and in particular Mario Kempes, had their scoring boots on again in the decider, beating the Dutch 3-1 after extra-time to the delight of the Estadio Monumental crowd. Argentina had broken their World Cup duck and South America had maintained its stranglehold of the tournament in its own backyard.

The 1978 World Cup is remembered for its ticker tape – and hurled toilet rolls!

THE BIG WORLD CUP GUIDE

CONTENTS

THE STADIUMS 40

THE COUNTRIES

SUPERSTARS OF BRAZIL

THE BEST OF BRAZIL

The 2014 World Cup will show off the best of Brazil – from north to south and east to west.

The 64 matches will be played at 12 venues in 12 host cities – that is two more stadiums and three more cities than at the previous World Cup in South Africa. Each setting promises to be spectacular, with every stadium either brand new or having undergone significant renovation, although fulfilling this commitment brought its own problems for the organisers.

The Maracana always has someone looking over it

At the time of publication, six stadiums were running behind schedule and had missed the FIFA deadline (as you will see from the photos over the pages that follow), arousing the wrath of football's world governing body and the chance that they might be withdrawn from the tournament if not completed.

Assuming they are ready on time, the host cities will show off far-flung areas of a country which stretches across half of South America. Situated in the Amazon basin, the Arena Amazonia in Manaus, where England will get their campaign underway against Italy, is the most northerly of all the venues and almost 2,000 miles from the Estadio Beira-Rio in Porto Alegre near neighbouring Uruguay. The Arena Pantanal in Cuiaba, meanwhile, is smack bang in the middle of the continent and close to the Bolivian border.

For most fans, day trips will be out of the question. The shortest distance between cities is the 250-mile journey from Sao Paulo to Curitiba, meaning flying will be the most efficient – if not the cheapest – mode of transport.

Italy, who will set up base in Rio de Janeiro, will clock in excess of 8,000 miles for their group games alone. France, on the other hand, have a much kinder schedule, with games relatively close together in Porto Alegre, Salvador and Rio, something which brought a smile to the face of their coach Didier Deschamps. "We stay more or less in the same area, which is not too far from our training camp. It's rather good news," he said.

Travelling supporters should pack brollies with their Bermuda shorts with significant changes in the climate from city to city. Four stadiums including the Maracana are at sea level, whereas the Estadio Nacional and Arena da Baixada are more than 3,000 feet above it. June and July may be winter months in Brazil, but that doesn't necessarily mean it will be woolly-jumper weather. While temperatures in Porto Alegre go down to 10 degrees and Curitiba has been known to get snow, further north in Cuiaba the mercury can rise to 37 degrees at this time of year. Brasilia and Sao Paulo are very dry, but in Recife it rains on average 224 days a year – to put it into perspective, that's more than double the annual rainfall in Manchester.

All told, such variables will cause some serious headaches for the 32 coaches in their preparations. Spare a thought for Honduras who must go from the cold of Curitiba to the heat of Manaus just five days later. With temperatures in the Amazon expected to be around 30 degrees, plus plenty of humidity, both England and Italy requested extra drinks breaks for their match once the draw was made.

The USA can expect a wide range of conditions on top of plenty of time in transit with games in Manaus, Natal and Recife. However, as their coach Jurgen Klinsmann explained, such challenges are what make the World Cup so special.

"It is what it is. We don't complain. We take it on. We do the travelling and we adjust to the climate. This is what a World Cup is about, it's about these challenges," he said. "It's exciting in certain ways, and a big challenge. That's what we want."

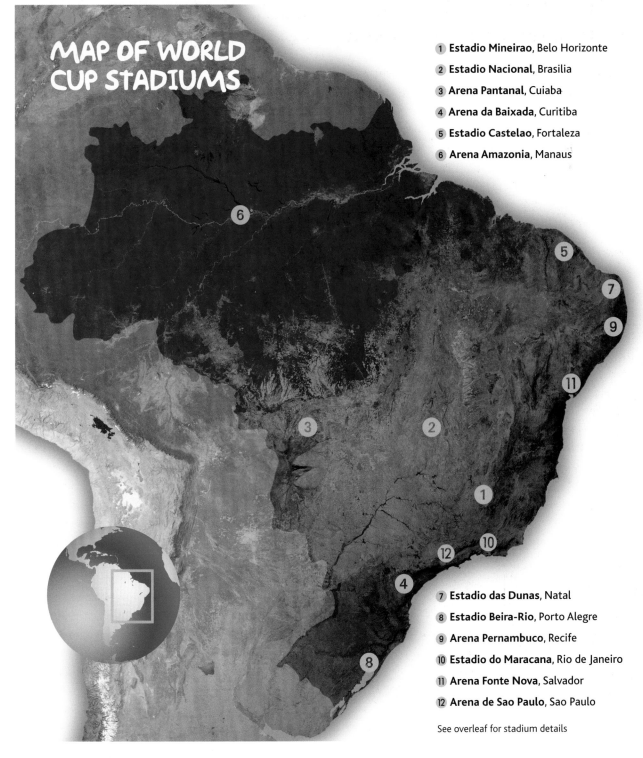

MAP OF WORLD CUP STADIUMS

1. **Estadio Mineirao**, Belo Horizonte
2. **Estadio Nacional**, Brasilia
3. **Arena Pantanal**, Cuiaba
4. **Arena da Baixada**, Curitiba
5. **Estadio Castelao**, Fortaleza
6. **Arena Amazonia**, Manaus

7. **Estadio das Dunas**, Natal
8. **Estadio Beira-Rio**, Porto Alegre
9. **Arena Pernambuco**, Recife
10. **Estadio do Maracana**, Rio de Janeiro
11. **Arena Fonte Nova**, Salvador
12. **Arena de Sao Paulo**, Sao Paulo

See overleaf for stadium details

❶ ESTADIO MINEIRAO
BELO HORIZONTE

Capacity: 62,547
First built: 1965
Matches: Group games, second round, semi-final

The famous Estadio Mineirao has played host to no shortage of historic matches over the past 50 years, involving either the Brazilian national team or club sides Cruzeiro and Atletico Mineiro who are based at the stadium. Another historic chapter seems guaranteed in 2014 with six World Cup games to be played at the venue, including England's final group game against Costa Rica. The Estadio Mineirao – which is a listed national monument – has undergone significant reconstruction and has a specially lowered playing surface to improve the spectator experience.

❷ ESTADIO NACIONAL
BRASILIA

Capacity: 68,009
First built: 1974
Matches: Group games, second round, quarter-final, 3rd/4th place play-off

Of the stadiums that will be on show this summer, only the Maracana has a bigger capacity than the Estadio Nacional. The venue is arguably also the most eye-catching, the circular design making it instantly recognisable across the Brasilia skyline. Since redevelopment, the stadium reopened for the 2013 Confederations Cup and has also proved popular in music circles, with Beyonce and Aerosmith both performing in the country's capital. A quarter-final and the 3rd/4th place play-off will be among seven matches to be held at the venue.

The nickname 'The Big Green' is particularly fitting for the Arena Pantanal. As with many of the new World Cup venues, sustainability played a major part in the construction of the Cuiaba stadium, with a key focus on recycling any building waste that was produced during the creation of the arena. The multi-use venue will not only stage football matches – there will be four group games in Cuiaba in June, including the clash between Japan and Colombia (possible second-round opponents for England) – but also play host to shows and exhibitions as part of its World Cup legacy.

③ ARENA PANTANAL
CUIABA

Capacity: 42,968
First built: 2014
Matches: Group games

The oldest original stadium of the 12 World Cup venues, the Arena da Baixada celebrates its centenary in 2014. It was renovated at the end of the last century and has undergone further work since being confirmed as a tournament host, but was running so far behind schedule in early 2014 that FIFA issued an ultimatum for completion of the construction. The capacity will be increased to more than 40,000 for the four group games which include France's opener against Nigeria. Located in the southern city of Curitiba, the Arena da Baixada is home to Atletico Paranaense.

④ ARENA DA BAIXADA
CURITIBA

Capacity: 41,456
First built: 1914
Matches: Group games

⑤ ESTADIO CASTELAO
FORTALEZA

Capacity: 64,846
First built: 1973
Matches: Group games, second round, quarter-final

The eyes of all of Brazil will be on the tourist hotspot of Fortaleza when the Samba boys come to town for their second group match against Mexico. The stadium is no stranger to being in the national spotlight as this was where star striker Ronaldo made his long-awaited return from injury before the 2002 World Cup. Having undergone an impressive reconstruction since then, which includes the addition of an eye-catching roof, the Estadio Castelao will host six matches in all this summer, with four group games and two knockout ties.

⑥ ARENA AMAZONIA
MANAUS

Capacity: 42,374
First built: 2014
Matches: Group games

The visually spectacular Arena Amazonia is situated in Manaus, the Amazon's largest city which is based in the middle of the rainforest. The stunning metal pattern that surrounds the exterior of the stadium represents a straw basket, a well-known product from the region. Sustainability is a major theme of the Arena Amazonia, with special initiatives – such as the collecting of rainwater to water the pitch – incorporated into the overall design. The stadium will stage four group games, including England's crucial first match against European rivals Italy.

In order to meet the hosting requirements for the 2014 World Cup, Natal needed to build a new, modern stadium. The result is the jaw-dropping Estadio das Dunas. The futuristic stadium design (its name and undulating shape are inspired by the sand dunes for which Natal is famed) was the brainchild of an architect from Populous, the company behind Wembley Stadium and the London 2012 Olympic Stadium, to name just a few. Four group games will be played at the Estadio das Dunas, including the match between England's group rivals, Italy and Uruguay.

⑦ ESTADIO DAS DUNAS
NATAL

Capacity: 42,086
First built: 2014
Matches: Group games

Known as the 'Gigante do Beira-Rio', the Estadio Beira-Rio in Porto Alegre certainly lives up to its giant nickname – with a capacity of almost 50,000 it is the biggest stadium in southern Brazil. Appropriately for a venue of such magnitude, it is home to one of Brazil's best-known clubs – Internacional. Originally constructed in 1969 with the assistance of Internacional's fans who donated building materials to the cause, the Estadio Beira-Rio has been redeveloped for the 2014 World Cup where it will stage four group games and a second-round match.

⑧ ESTADIO BEIRA-RIO
PORTO ALEGRE

Capacity: 48, 849
First built: 1969
Matches: Group games, second round

⑨ ARENA PERNAMBUCO

RECIFE

Capacity: 44,248
First built: 2013
Matches: Group games, second round

A traditional hotbed for Brazilian football, Recife is home to three of Brazil's most famous clubs, Nautico, Sport and Santa Cruz. In 2014, the city fittingly has a new stadium for the world's biggest football tournament, in which it will host five games including the highly fancied Germans against the USA and a second-round match featuring the winner of England's pool, Group D. Situated in Recife's western suburbs, the multi-purpose Arena Pernambuco was built as part of a project to develop the area and has been the home ground for Nautico since 2013.

⑩ ESTADIO DO MARACANA RIO DE JANEIRO

Capacity: 76,804
First built: 1950
Matches: Group games, second round, quarter-final, final

The venue for the 1950 World Cup decider between Brazil and Uruguay, the Maracana will once again host the final match at the 2014 World Cup. Once the biggest sports stadium in the world with a capacity of almost 200,000, it has been redeveloped for the tournament, with England's 2-2 draw against Brazil in June 2013 the first official match at the new venue. The Maracana, which will stage seven World Cup games including Argentina's opener against Bosnia-Hercegovina, remains one of the most popular tourist attractions in Rio de Janeiro.

A favourite destination for holidaymakers, Salvador is known for its music, cuisine and fun-loving lifestyle. There is sure to be a carnival atmosphere when the city welcomes fans for six games at the Arena Fonte Nova, including the blockbuster between Spain and the Netherlands. The redeveloped stadium, designed by German architects who worked on the 2006 World Cup, replaced the Estadio Fonte Nova. Builders used 92 per cent of the rubble from the old venue to create the new stadium which stands out with its distinctive horse-shoe design.

⑪ ARENA FONTE NOVA
SALVADOR

Capacity: 48,747
First built: 1951
Matches: Group games, second round, quarter-final

A newly constructed stadium, the Arena de Sao Paulo will be the home of one of the biggest and most popular Brazilian clubs, Corinthians. The venue, which will contain 20,000 extra temporary seats for the World Cup, has the honour of staging the opening match of the tournament between Brazil and Croatia and will host five other games, including a semi-final. In contrast to the stifling conditions in Manaus, England can expect relatively cool temperatures for their second group match against Luis Suarez and Uruguay.

⑫ ARENA DE SAO PAULO
SAO PAULO

Capacity: 65, 807
First built: 2014
Matches: Group games, second round, semi-final

BRAZIL

As hosts of this summer's finals Brazil can count on their noisy, colourful and passionate fans playing their part as the five-time World Cup winners attempt to wrestle the trophy from the grasp of holders Spain. The South Americans, though, have a lot more going for them than mere home advantage and with a team packed full of star names, including pin-up boy Neymar, they will fancy their chances of winning the tournament.

Any doubts about Brazil's ability to match the sky-high expectations of their supporters were shattered at the 2013 Confederations Cup, when they swaggered to victory playing a brand of vibrant attacking football that simply swept their opponents aside. The emphatic 3-0 victory over Spain in the final, secured by two goals from Fluminense striker Fred and a Neymar special, was particularly impressive.

> **"We can't worry too far ahead past the group stage. We have to worry about these teams first."**
>
> Brazil coach
> Luiz Felipe Scolari

However, coach Luiz Felipe Scolari won't be getting carried away. He will know that his team is still a work in progress. He might harbour doubts about the lack of playing time at club level for first-choice goalkeeper Julio Cesar and also about playing frizzy-haired Chelsea defender David Luiz at centre-back where his sometimes rash decision-making can prove costly.

On the other hand, Scolari has numerous reasons to feel confident. He has some wonderful players in his side – including the brilliant Neymar, Chelsea midfielder Oscar and his captain, rugged Paris Saint-Germain defender Thiago Silva – and he has settled on a 4-3-3 system that perfectly suits the disparate talents available to him. He can also count on the yellow-shirted hordes in the stadiums creating a hostile atmosphere that will put most opponents on the back foot right from the start.

No wonder then that Brazil are the bookies' favourites this summer. They are going to take some stopping.

THE GAFFER: LUIZ FELIPE SCOLARI

The Brazilian nation expects nothing less than victory at the World Cup this summer, and in Luiz Felipe Scolari the country has a manager who knows how to deliver the ultimate triumph following his success with the Selecao in Japan and South Korea in 2002.

Since then the moustachioed Gene Hackman-lookalike has further embellished his already impressive CV, which included Copa Libertadores titles with Gremio and Palmeiras in the 1990s. Appointed Portugal manager in 2003 Scolari took the perennial European under-achievers to the final of the European Championships the following year, where they surprisingly lost on home soil to Greece, and to the semi-finals of the 2006 World Cup in Germany.

After leaving the Portugal job in 2008 he was appointed Chelsea boss – becoming the Premier League's first ever World Cup-winning manager. A good start was soon undermined by the Brazilian's tactical inflexibility and he was sacked by Roman Abramovich in February 2009. After brief spells with Uzbekistan champions Bunyodkor – on a reported salary of £11 million a year – and Palmeiras, Scolari became Brazil boss for a second time in November 2012.

His first year in charge brought the 2013 Confederations Cup in fine style, but a much bigger challenge lies ahead.

KEY PLAYER

OSCAR

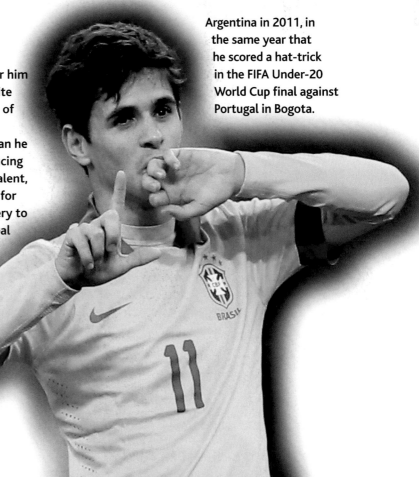

He may have the cherubic features and skinny physique of a 14-year-old choirboy but Brazil midfielder Oscar has a man-sized job lined up for him this summer at the World Cup finals – and, despite his apparent weediness, he is more than capable of excelling at it.

The Chelsea star is actually much stronger than he initially appears, sometimes winning wince-inducing challenges with much bigger players. His main talent, though, is on the ball, whether creating chances for others with a deft pass, using his pace and trickery to take on defenders, or shooting powerfully for goal from just outside the box.

Oscar, whose full name is Oscar dos Santos Emboaba Junior, started out with Sao Paulo before moving to Internacional in 2010. He joined Chelsea two years later in a £19.35 million deal and helped the Blues win the Europa League in his first season at Stamford Bridge.

He made his senior debut for Brazil against Argentina in 2011, in the same year that he scored a hat-trick in the FIFA Under-20 World Cup final against Portugal in Bogota.

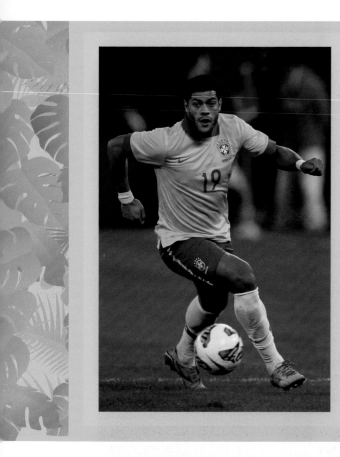

ONE TO WATCH: HULK

A direct, powerfully-built flank player who loves to cut inside to unleash a fierce shot, Hulk is a key man in Brazil's three-pronged attack.

Born Givanildo Vieira de Souza in 1986, Hulk moved early in his career to Japan to play for Kawasaki Frontale. It was in the Far East that he acquired his nickname, thanks to his barrel chest, square jaw and frequent angry glares at opponents, referees and under-performing team-mates.

In 2008 Hulk joined Porto and went on to enjoy huge success with the Portuguese giants, averaging a goal every other game and winning three league titles as well as the Europa League in 2011.

The following year he joined Zenit Saint Petersburg in a massive £50 million deal, but his vast wages were resented by some less well-paid players. For a while, it appeared that his stay in Russia would be a short one and he was linked throughout 2013 with a number of top European clubs.

Hulk made his debut for Brazil in a friendly win against England in Doha in 2009 and in 2013 he was an ever-present in his country's Confederations Cup victory.

TACTICS BOARD
ALL OUT ATTACK

Brazil coach Luiz Felipe Scolari laid his cards on the table at the 2013 Confederations Cup, setting his team out in an offensive 4-3-3 system and only making one change to his starting XI in five matches.

The South Americans' front three are all genuine attackers with vastly different attributes: Neymar on the left is fast and tricky; Hulk on the right is built like a tank and has a powerful left-foot shot; and central striker Fred is a goal poacher who comes alive in the penalty area.

The trio in midfield also have contrasting roles. Twinkle-toed Oscar is the creative playmaker, Paulinho is an energetic runner and scrapper, and Wolfsburg's Luiz Gustavo is the sitting player who rarely ventures into the final third.

The two full-backs, Barcelona's Dani Alves and Real Madrid's Marcelo, also spend most of their time beyond the halfway line, which can leave Brazil exposed to swift counter-attacks.

BRAZIL AT THE WORLD CUP

• Brazil first competed at the World Cup in 1930, but failed to get out of their group after losing 2-1 to Yugoslavia. However, the South Americans did record their first win at the finals with a 4-0 hammering of Bolivia.

• **As hosts in 1950 Brazil only needed to draw with Uruguay in the last match of the final four-team pool to win the trophy for the first time. Filled to bursting point, the Maracana Stadium in Rio erupted when the home side took the lead just after half-time, but Uruguay responded with two goals to pip Brazil to the title.**

• The Brazilians finally got their hands on the trophy in 1958 when they beat hosts Sweden 5-2 in the final in Stockholm. Two of their goals were scored by an unknown 17-year-old striker called Pele, who became the youngest ever World Cup winner.

• **Four years later Brazil retained their trophy in Chile, beating Czechoslovakia 3-1 in the final in Santiago. The Brazilians' star player was winger Garrincha, who had overcome polio as a child to become a dazzling, if slightly bow-legged, dribbler.**

• A brilliantly flamboyant Brazilian side containing the likes of Pele, skipper Carlos Alberto and midfield maestro Gerson won the trophy

Ronaldinho keeps a tight grip on the World Cup in 2002

for an unprecedented third time in Mexico in 1970. Flying winger Jairzinho scored in every round, including a 4-1 demolition of Italy in the final – a feat no player has matched since.

• **After an agonising 24-year wait, Brazil won the World Cup for a fourth time in the USA in 1994. Again, Italy were their opponents in the final, but this time the South Americans only tasted victory after the penalty shoot-out following a sterile 0-0 draw.**

• A record fifth trophy followed in 2002 when Brazil beat Germany 2-0 in the final in Yokohama. Gap-

toothed striker Ronaldo helped himself to both goals and, at the next tournament in Germany, took his total World Cup tally to a record 15 goals, one ahead of Gerd Muller.

• **The only country to appear at all 19 previous finals, Brazil were among the favourites to triumph at the last World Cup in South Africa. They got off to a good start, topping a difficult group and then beating Chile 3-0 in the last 16. The South Americans led the Netherlands at half-time in their quarter-final tie, but then conceded twice in a disappointing second-half performance to crash out of the tournament.**

PREVIOUS TOURNAMENTS

1930 Round 1	1966 Round 1	1994 Winners
1934 Round 1	1970 Winners	1998 Runners-up
1938 Semi-finals	1974 Fourth place	2002 Winners
1950 Runners-up	1978 Third place	2006 Quarter-finals
1954 Quarter-finals	1982 Round 2	2010 Quarter-finals
1958 Winners	1986 Quarter-finals	
1962 Winners	1990 Round 2	

CROATIA

Of all the nations heading to Brazil, Croatia qualified in arguably the least impressive fashion. After picking up just one point in their last four group games the Balkan country limped into the play-offs, where they struggled to overcome a mediocre Iceland side over two legs. Nevertheless, Croatia are not to be underestimated and if they play to their full potential could be a team to watch at the finals.

The Croatians' poor form towards the end of their qualifying campaign, which included defeats to Scotland home and away, led to the dismissal of unpopular manager Igor Stimac and his replacement by former international Niko Kovac, just a few weeks before the crucial play-off decider. Aged just 42, Kovac is a novice coach but already appears to have created an improved team spirit in the Croatian camp.

> "We will do everything to prepare for the opener against the hosts."
>
> Croatia coach
> Niko Kovac

In Brazil he will rely on a core of players who have served the national team well for many years. In goal Stipe Pletikosa is a vastly experienced figure with more than 100 caps under his belt, while veteran Shakhtar Donetsk defender Darijo Srna is also a member of the centurions' club.

Further forward, Real Madrid's mercurial midfielder Luka Modric is one of the most creative and visionary talents in the European game, and he will be supported by Seville's Ivan Rakitic and the exciting Mateo Kovacic, a brilliantly gifted playmaker with Inter Milan who is tipped to become a star of the future.

Despite scoring a paltry 12 goals in their 10 group games, Croatia have a number of useful attacking options. Bayern Munich's Mario Mandzukic is their most potent striking force, but as he will miss the start of the tournament through suspension there could be a starting place for either Hull City's Nikica Jelavic or former Arsenal striker Eduardo, now with Shakhtar Donetsk.

CROATIA AT THE WORLD CUP

• Formerly a part of Yugoslavia, Croatia first competed at the World Cup in France in 1998. They did remarkably well, too, smashing Germany 3-0 in the quarter-finals in one of the biggest shocks in World Cup history. In the semi-finals Croatia took the lead against the hosts but were eventually beaten 2-1 and had to be satisfied with third place. With six goals, Croatia striker Davor Suker was top scorer at the tournament.

• **The Croatians fared less well at the 2002 tournament, although a 2-1 victory over Italy in their second group game appeared to set them on course for the last 16. However, a surprise 1-0 defeat by Ecuador ended their hopes of reaching the knockout phase.**

• On their last appearance at the finals in 2006 Croatia needed to beat Australia in their final group game to progress to the second round. In a dramatic encounter, though, they were held to a 2-2 draw which ended in bizarre circumstances when Croatia's Josip Simunic was only sent off by English referee Graham Poll after being shown three yellow cards.

PREVIOUS TOURNAMENTS

1930-90 Competed as part of Yugoslavia	1998 Third place	2010 Did not qualify
1994 Could not enter	2002 Round 1	
	2006 Round 1	

KEY PLAYER

MARIO MANDZUKIC

A prolific goalscorer who never gives defenders a moment's peace, Mario Mandzukic will be Croatia's main attacking threat in Brazil.

The Bayern Munich striker will also go into the tournament on a high after enjoying a hugely successful year in 2013, the highlight being the goal he scored in the Champions League final which helped the Bavarian club beat German rivals Borussia Dortmund 2-1 at Wembley.

That triumph capped a remarkable treble for Mandzukic who, in his first season with Bayern following his arrival from Wolfsburg, also won the Bundesliga title and the German Cup. The previous campaign hadn't been a bad one either for the hitman as he was voted Croatian Footballer of the Year after finishing joint-top scorer at the 2012 European Championships with three goals, including a double against the Republic of Ireland in the group stage.

Replicating that impressive feat this summer will be tough, especially as Mandzukic will miss Croatia's first match against Brazil through suspension after being sent off in the second leg of the play-off against Iceland.

MEXICO

When Mexico beat Brazil 2-1 in the final of the 2012 Olympic football tournament few of their fans could have anticipated that their heroes would struggle to reach the World Cup finals just two years later. However, that's exactly what happened as the Central Americans endured a nightmare campaign, only booking their place in Brazil after an emphatic play-off victory against New Zealand.

Mexico's dismal form in the final CONCACAF group – they only won two of their 10 games and limped into fourth place some way behind the USA, Costa Rica and Honduras – resulted in three coaches getting the boot, before Miguel Herrera took over for the two-legged duel with the Kiwis.

> "Mexico always gives Brazil indigestion."
>
> Mexico coach Miguel Herrera is not unhappy at drawing the hosts

Previously the boss of reigning Mexico title winners America, Herrera made the radical decision to choose only home-based players for the play-off double header. The strategy worked perfectly, with the Mexicans cruising to a spectacular 9-3 aggregate win which made a mockery of their disappointing earlier performances.

Santos Laguna striker Oribe Peralta, who scored both the gold medal-winning goals at Wembley, helped himself to four goals against New Zealand and his partnership with Manchester United's Javier Hernandez will be key to Mexican hopes in Brazil. Herrera has indicated that the overseas players will return to the squad for the finals, so that should mean starting slots for Ajaccio goalkeeper Guilermo Ochoa, Espanyol defender Hector Moreno, Valencia's exciting left-sided midfielder Andres Guardado and former Tottenham Hotspur midfielder Giovani dos Santos, now with Villarreal.

Following Mexico's haphazard and unconvincing qualification campaign, it is difficult to assess their chances in Brazil. However, they have a decent World Cup record in recent times, reaching the second round at the last five tournaments, and they may well progress from the group stage yet again.

MEXICO AT THE WORLD CUP

• Mexico were the first country to host the World Cup twice. In 1970 they took advantage of playing on home soil to reach the quarter-finals for the first time in their history, at which stage they lost 4-1 to Italy. The Mexicans repeated that feat in 1986, when they filled in for the original host nation, Colombia. This time West Germany knocked them out on penalties after a deadly dull 0-0 draw.

• **FIFA banned Mexico from the 1990 tournament after the Central Americans fielded over-age players in the qualifiers for the 1988 Olympics.**

• Since then the Mexicans have been extremely consistent, reaching the last 16 at the previous five World Cups, including the 2010 tournament in South Africa when they were knocked out by Argentina – a defeat which led coach Javier Aguirre to resign afterwards.

• **Mexico goalkeeper Antonio Carbajal was the first player to appear at five consecutive World Cups, featuring for his country in the 1950, 1954, 1958, 1962 and 1966 tournaments. Less impressively, he conceded a record 25 goals in the 11 matches he played in.**

PREVIOUS TOURNAMENTS

1930 Round 1	1966 Round 1	1994 Round 2
1934 Did not qualify	1970 Quarter-finals	1998 Round 2
1938 Withdrew	1974 Did not qualify	2002 Round 2
1950 Round 1	1978 Round 1	2006 Round 2
1954 Round 1	1982 Did not qualify	2010 Round 2
1958 Round 1	1986 Quarter-finals	
1962 Round 1	1990 Banned	

KEY PLAYER

JAVIER HERNANDEZ

A crafty goal poacher who is adept at finding space even in the most crowded of penalty areas, Javier Hernandez is the third highest scorer in Mexico's history despite making his international debut just five years ago.

Known as 'Chicarito' ('Little Pea'), Hernandez rose to prominence at the 2010 World Cup in South Africa, scoring goals against France and Argentina. The following year he starred at the CONCACAF Gold Cup, helping Mexico beat the USA 4-2 in the final and finishing the tournament as the top scorer with seven goals.

Hernandez's impressive feats with Mexico brought him to the attention of Europe's leading clubs and in 2010 he moved from Guadalajara to Manchester United for £8 million. He has since helped United win two league titles, although he has found a regular first-team place difficult to secure and has mostly been used as an impact substitute.

CAMEROON

Cameroon are World Cup veterans and will make their seventh appearance at the finals in Brazil – a record no other African side can match. Although the Indomitable Lions have only once progressed beyond the group stages, when they famously beat Argentina in the opening match at Italia '90, they always provide stiff opposition and there is every reason to believe they will do the same this summer.

The Africans' progress to the finals was fairly comfortable, and confirmed when they beat Tunisia 4-1 on aggregate in the play-offs. Along the way, though, they changed coaches, German Volker Finke taking charge halfway through the qualification process. The former Freiburg and Urawa Red Diamonds boss likes to play with two strong holding midfielders in front of his defence, and will be able to field two good ones in Brazil in the form of Barcelona's Alex Song and Stephane Mbia, currently on loan at Sevilla from QPR. Alongside this duo, former Aston Villa midfielder Jean Makoun, now with French side Rennes, will be charged with a more attacking and creative role.

> "When you play Brazil you're up against the emotion of the whole country."
>
> Cameroon coach Volker Finke

Further forward, Cameroon will look to Chelsea's Samuel Eto'o to snap up the chances that come his way. He certainly knows where the net is, having averaged a goal every other game in more than 100 international appearances. Eto'o will probably be supported by the equally experienced Pierre Webo of Fenerbahce, although another option for Finke to consider is exciting young Mainz striker Eric Maxim Choupo-Moting.

There's no doubt that Cameroon have the ability to score goals but their defence, which could well include former Tottenham team-mates Benoit Assou-Ekotto and Sebastien Bassong, may struggle to keep clean sheets. In a group which will in all likelihood be won by Brazil, much will depend on how the Indomitable Lions' rearguard copes against Croatia and Mexico.

CAMEROON AT THE WORLD CUP

• Cameroon impressed at their first World Cup in 1982, holding eventual winners Italy 1-1 and drawing all three of their group games. However, they just missed out on a second-round place on goals scored.

• The Indomitable Lions fared even better at their next finals in 1990, sensationally beating reigning champions Argentina 1-0 in the tournament's opening fixture, despite having two players sent off. With veteran striker Roger Milla to the fore, Cameroon marched on to the quarter-finals, where they lost 3-2 to England in a thrilling encounter.

• Milla became the oldest player ever to appear at the finals, when he played for the Africans at the 1994 tournament in the USA at the age of 42. When he scored Cameroon's consolation goal in a 6-1 mauling by Russia he claimed the record as the oldest goalscorer at the finals.

• Cameroon disappointed on their last World Cup appearance in South Africa in 2010, losing all three of their group games to Japan, Denmark and the Netherlands to finish bottom of their group.

PREVIOUS TOURNAMENTS

1930 Did not enter	1966 Withdrew	1994 Round 1
1934 Did not enter	1970 Did not qualify	1998 Round 1
1938 Did not enter	1974 Did not qualify	2002 Round 1
1950 Did not enter	1978 Did not qualify	2006 Did not qualify
1954 Did not enter	1982 Round 1	2010 Round 1
1958 Did not enter	1986 Did not qualify	
1962 Did not enter	1990 Quarter-finals	

KEY PLAYER

SAMUEL ETO'O

A striker who can pounce panther-like when a goalscoring opportunity arises, Samuel Eto'o is an absolute legend of African football.

After making his debut for Cameroon while still 15 in 1997, Eto'o has gone on to become his country's leading all-time scorer and the highest ever scorer in the African Cup of Nations – a competition he has helped his nation win on two occasions. He has played in three previous World Cups, scoring three times. His magnificent goalscoring feats have seen him crowned African Player of the Year a record four times, most recently in 2010.

Eto'o's achievements in club football are equally remarkable. He won the Champions League with Barcelona in 2006 and 2009 and Inter Milan in 2010, scoring against Arsenal and Manchester United to become only the second player to find the net in two finals.

After a stint with Russian side Anzhi Makhachkala, Eto'o made a surprise move to Chelsea in August 2013.

SPAIN

Having won the World Cup in 2010 and the European Championships in both 2008 and 2012, Spain are aiming for an unprecedented 'Double Double' of major international titles this summer. It won't be easy, though, especially as the Spanish have been drawn in the same group as the Netherlands, the team they beat in the final in South Africa. Nonetheless, their unrivalled big-game experience and strength in depth make them one of the tournament favourites.

Spain will go into the finals in reasonably good form. They qualified comfortably enough, remaining unbeaten in their eight group games. Less impressively, on the other hand, they suffered a heavy 3-0 defeat to hosts Brazil in the final of the 2013 Confederations Cup. Worryingly, they could meet Brazil again as early as the last 16 – in all likelihood if they finish second in their group – a prospect that doesn't appeal much to Spain's long-serving coach, Vicente del Bosque.

His team should be capable of avoiding that nightmare scenario. From back to front Spain ooze class, talent and quality. Goalkeeper Iker Casillas is still one of the best shot-stoppers in the business, while a defence featuring the likes of Sergio Ramos and Gerard Pique is rarely breached.

It's in midfield, though, that Spain's greatest strength lies, with the Barcelona trio of Sergio Busquets, Xavi and Andres Iniesta adept at monopolising possession for long periods. Ahead of them, Manchester City's bustling striker Alvaro Negredo and tricky wide man David Silva have a superb understanding, while Barca's Pedro also poses a genuine goal threat.

So, can Spain make it four major tournament wins on the trot? There's no doubt that they are still a great side, but some of their star performers are now well into their thirties and this may be the tournament where their ageing legs just start to creak a little.

> **"We can't say we were handed an easy draw. It's a complicated group with tough sides."**
>
> Spain coach
> Vicente del Bosque

THE GAFFER: VICENTE DEL BOSQUE

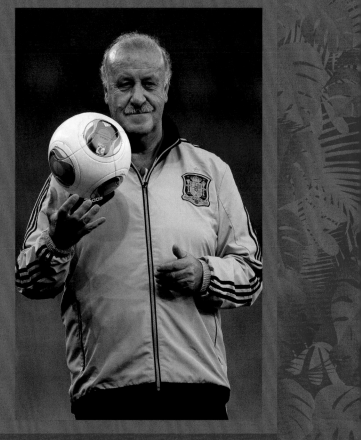

One of the most successful managers in international football history, Vicente del Bosque has led Spain to success in both the World Cup and European Championships since taking over as national team coach in 2008.

A dead ringer for cafe owner Rene in the popular TV sitcom 'Allo 'Allo!, the moustachioed Del Bosque got off to a great start as Spain boss when he won his first 13 matches in charge to set a new world record. Winning the World Cup in 2010 was an even more impressive feat, after which he was raised to the Spanish nobility by an appreciative King Juan Carlos, becoming the 1st Marquis of Del Bosque. In 2012 he guided Spain to the European Championships and shortly afterwards was named FIFA World Coach of the Year.

Previously, Del Bosque was a long-term servant of Real Madrid, initially as a defensive midfielder in the 1970s and 1980s and then as a coach at various levels. In 1999 he became manager of the Spanish giants, and went on to lead them to two Champions League titles before being unceremoniously sacked just days after securing a second La Liga title in 2003. He later had a short spell with Turkish club Besiktas.

KEY PLAYER

XAVI

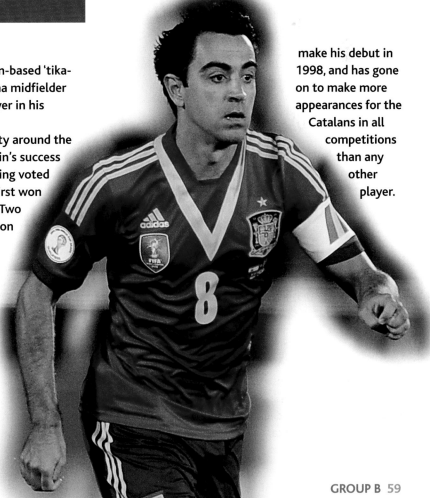

The beating heart of Spain's possession-based 'tika-taka' style of play, diminutive Barcelona midfielder Xavi is the second-highest capped player in his country's history.

Xavi's accurate passing and creativity around the box have been key components of Spain's success in recent years, with the Barca man being voted Player of the Tournament when they first won the European Championships in 2008. Two years later he starred again as Spain won the World Cup, and in 2012 Xavi made it a hat-trick of international honours when he helped his country retain the Euros. Once more, Xavi was a hugely influential figure in the tournament, making more passes than any other player and setting up two goals in the final as Spain thrashed Italy 4-0.

At club level, Xavi has won a vast amount of silverware with Barcelona, including a multitude of La Liga and Champions League titles. Now 34, he came through the youth ranks to make his debut in 1998, and has gone on to make more appearances for the Catalans in all competitions than any other player.

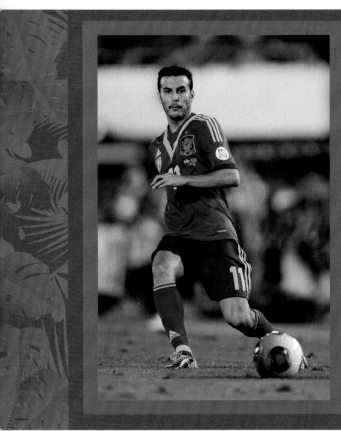

ONE TO WATCH: PEDRO

Despite being one of the most consistent performers in world football, Barcelona winger Pedro is something of an unsung hero, rarely featuring in the headlines dominated by some of his more famous team-mates.

He may be underrated by the media, but there's no doubting Pedro's quality. Fast, deceptively strong and equally adept with his right and left foot, there is nothing especially fancy or flamboyant about the 26-year-old, but he adds a dash of much-needed directness to a Spanish team which can be guilty of over-elaboration. He has a pretty good goalscoring record, too, averaging better than a goal every four games for both club and country.

Born in Tenerife, Pedro came through the Barcelona youth ranks to become a regular in the first team in 2009/10, a season in which he set a world record by scoring in six different official club competitions. Having played a bit part in Barca's 2009 Champions League success, he starred in their 2011 triumph, scoring in the final against Manchester United at Wembley.

Pedro made his Spain debut in 2010, going on to play in that year's World Cup final against the Netherlands in South Africa.

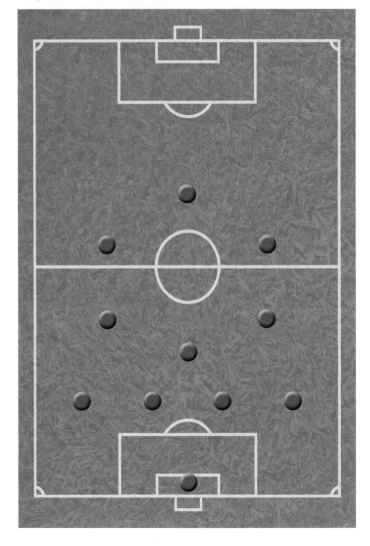

TACTICS BOARD
POSSESSION PLAY

Spain coach Vicente del Bosque has occasionally played without a striker over the last couple of years, but his controversial 4-6-0 formation has had mixed results and is unlikely to be seen in Brazil.

Instead, Del Bosque is likely to set up the world champions in a 4-3-3 system that makes the best use of Spain's abundance of talent in midfield. With Sergio Busquets holding in front of the back four, his Barcelona team-mates Xavi and Andres Iniesta set the tempo of Spain's attack with their unerringly accurate passing. Manchester City's David Silva and Barcelona's Pedro provide the main threat on the wings, supported by energetic full-backs Jordi Alba and Alvaro Arbeloa, while the sometimes troublesome lone striker's position will probably be filled by another City player, Alvaro Negredo.

At the back Sergio Ramos and Gerard Pique are a steady pair, with the latter particularly adept at bringing the ball out of defence.

SPAIN AT THE WORLD CUP

• Spain's first ever World Cup match saw them defeat Brazil 3-1 in 1934. Their next game with hosts Italy went to a replay before the injury-hit Spanish went down to a 1-0 defeat.

• **Spain enjoyed better fortune at the 1950 tournament in Brazil, beating the USA, Chile and England to enter the final pool of four teams. After a satisfactory opening 2-2 draw with eventual winners Uruguay, the Spanish were crushed 6-1 by Brazil and 3-1 by Sweden to finish fourth.**

• With Real Madrid dominating the European Cup in the late 1950s and early 1960s, Spain might have been expected to be a real force during this era. However, the Spanish made little impression at the World Cup, failing to qualify for the 1958 tournament and going home after the group stages in both 1962 and 1966.

• **As hosts in 1982, Spain fared a bit better while still leaving their fans feeling deeply frustrated. After suffering a humiliating 1-0 defeat by Northern Ireland in Valencia, the Spanish only scraped into the second round on goals scored. A 2-1 defeat to West Germany pretty much ended their chances of reaching the semi-finals, making their draw with Ron Greenwood's England side largely academic.**

Spain celebrate their first ever World Cup win in 2010

• Four years later Spain stormed into the quarter-finals thanks to a magnificent 5-1 demolition of Denmark in the last 16 in Mexico, with Real Madrid striker Emilio 'The Vulture' Butragueno hitting four of the goals. However, a penalty shoot-out defeat to Belgium in the last eight dashed their World Cup dreams once more.

• **Spain were beaten in the quarter-finals again in 1994 in the USA, losing 2-1 to Italy. After a disappointing showing in 1998, the Spanish once more made it to the last eight in 2002 before going down to co-hosts South Korea. Mind you, they were desperately unlucky to have two seemingly valid goals disallowed by the officials.**

• Spain's luck finally changed in South Africa in 2010 when they won the competition for the first time. Their campaign began badly with a shock 1-0 defeat to Switzerland, but they recovered to get through the group stage and then saw off Portugal, Paraguay and Germany before meeting the Netherlands in the final in Johannesburg. Refusing to be intimidated by the crudely physical tactics of the Dutch, Spain lifted the trophy thanks to an Andres Iniesta goal deep into extra-time.

PREVIOUS TOURNAMENTS

1930 Did not enter	1966 Round 1	1994 Quarter-finals
1934 Quarter-finals	1970 Did not qualify	1998 Round 1
1938 Did not enter	1974 Did not qualify	2002 Quarter-finals
1950 Fourth place	1978 Round 1	2006 Round 2
1954 Did not qualify	1982 Round 2	2010 Winners
1958 Did not qualify	1986 Quarter-finals	
1962 Round 1	1990 Round 2	

NETHERLANDS

The Netherlands were runners-up at the last World Cup in South Africa but their extremely physical, and at times brutally violent, approach in the final against Spain won them few friends – as well as a red card for defender Johnny Heitinga. Under current boss Louis van Gaal, though, the Dutch have changed their style and once again embraced the 'Total Football' philosophy that made Johan Cruyff, Johan Neeskens and co. a joy to watch in their 1970s heyday.

If the Dutch reproduce the form they showed in the qualifiers they will certainly entertain at the finals. Van Gaal's side were undefeated in their 10 games, only dropping points in a 2-2 draw away to Estonia and scoring 34 goals in total – a tally only bettered by Germany. Considering that the team was effectively in transition, with a number of young players being introduced, it was a remarkable record.

The influx of new faces is especially noticeable in the Dutch defence, with the likes of Feyenoord right-back Daryl Janmaat and his club team-mate Bruno Martins Indi establishing themselves in the side,

> **"The opponents are tough, but for the playing conditions it is not too bad."**
> Netherlands coach
> Louis van Gaal

playing in front of veteran Fulham goalkeeper Maarten Stekelenburg. Another recent addition is Roma's Kevin Strootman, a tough-tackling midfielder who is known as the 'Dutch Roy Keane'. Other midfield options for Van Gaal in his favoured 4-3-3 system include old hands Wesley Sneijder and Rafael van der Vaart and Norwich City's Leroy Fer.

Up front, the Netherlands possess two world-class forwards in Robin van Persie, top scorer in the European qualifying section with 11 goals, and Arjen Robben. Another new name, Dynamo Kiev's Jeremain Lens, is likely to complete an attacking trio that looks extremely strong.

The Dutch clearly have the firepower to do well in Brazil, but much will depend on their keenly anticipated rematch with Spain – especially as the runners-up in their group will probably face the hosts in the last 16.

THE GAFFER: LOUIS VAN GAAL

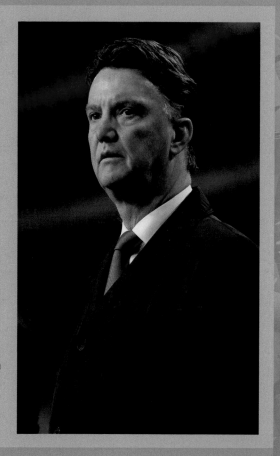

The Netherlands will have one of the most experienced coaches in the world in their dug-out this summer in the shape of Louis van Gaal.

Appointed in July 2012, the 62-year-old is in his second spell in charge of the Dutch, having previously held the post between 2000 and 2002. However, Van Gaal won't recall that time with any pleasure as it culminated in the Dutch failing to reach the finals of the 2002 World Cup after finishing third in their qualifying group behind Portugal and the Republic of Ireland.

Van Gaal's record in club football, though, is simply sensational. He has won the league title at least once with all four clubs he has managed – Ajax, Barcelona, AZ Alkmaar and Bayern Munich – and in the early 1990s led the Amsterdam outfit to victory in both the UEFA Cup and Champions League. He also took Bayern to the Champions League final in 2010, but they were beaten by Jose Mourinho's Inter Milan.

A journeyman midfielder in his playing days with Sparta Rotterdam, Van Gaal is a strong advocate of attacking football and known for his flexible tactical formations. Or as he puts it, "It's a football philosophy more than a system."

KEY PLAYER

ARJEN ROBBEN

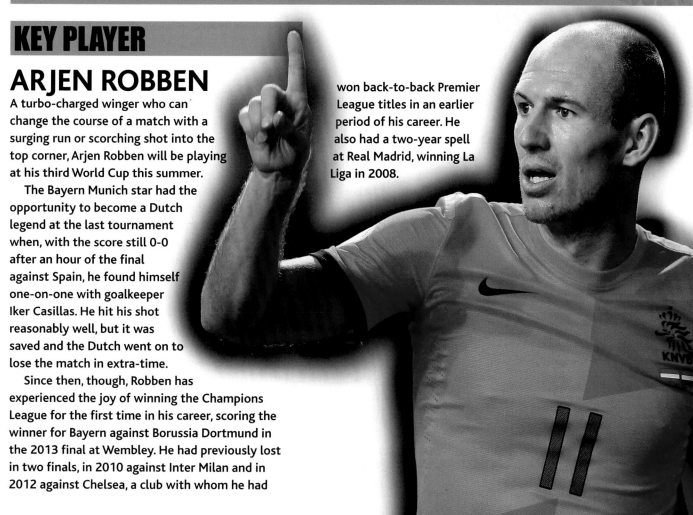

A turbo-charged winger who can change the course of a match with a surging run or scorching shot into the top corner, Arjen Robben will be playing at his third World Cup this summer.

The Bayern Munich star had the opportunity to become a Dutch legend at the last tournament when, with the score still 0-0 after an hour of the final against Spain, he found himself one-on-one with goalkeeper Iker Casillas. He hit his shot reasonably well, but it was saved and the Dutch went on to lose the match in extra-time.

Since then, though, Robben has experienced the joy of winning the Champions League for the first time in his career, scoring the winner for Bayern against Borussia Dortmund in the 2013 final at Wembley. He had previously lost in two finals, in 2010 against Inter Milan and in 2012 against Chelsea, a club with whom he had won back-to-back Premier League titles in an earlier period of his career. He also had a two-year spell at Real Madrid, winning La Liga in 2008.

ONE TO WATCH: JEREMAIN LENS

A pacy, energetic winger who can also play as a second striker, Jeremain Lens chipped in with five goals during the Netherlands' unbeaten qualifying campaign and impressed throughout with his work-rate, stamina and ability on the ball.

Now with Dynamo Kiev, the 26-year-old started out with AZ Alkmaar but struggled to establish himself in the team and played little part in his side's surprise league title triumph in 2009. His career picked up when he moved to PSV the following year, and he starred when the Eindhoven outfit won the Dutch Cup in 2012, scoring in the 3-0 defeat of Heracles in the final.

Although he was born in Amsterdam, Lens is of Surinamese origin and in 2009 accepted an offer to play for the Surinam national team. Fortunately, as it turned out, the tournament he appeared in was not recognised by FIFA and he was cleared by football's world governing body to play for the Netherlands the following year. After just missing out on the 2010 World Cup squad, Lens made his debut against Ukraine shortly afterwards, scoring in a 1-1 draw.

TACTICS BOARD
TOTAL FOOTBALL MKII

The Netherlands' strategic approach is neatly summed up by their coach Louis van Gaal, who says, "We do not like all the extreme passing and passing that Spain do. We want to do the business – score goals."

To that end, Van Gaal has adopted an offensive 4-3-3 system reminiscent of the 'Total Football' system the Dutch famously employed in the 1970s. The front three, usually Robin van Persie, Arjen Robben and Jeremain Lens, have the freedom to swap positions, although the Manchester United man is most likely to appear at the point of the attack. Behind them, former Tottenham star Rafael van der Vaart and the clever Wesley Sneijder, now with Galatasaray, are both attack-minded midfielders, leaving more defensive duties to Roma's Kevin Strootman.

At the back, question marks surround a young defence that is still unproven so don't be surprised if the Dutch are involved in some high-scoring games in Brazil.

NETHERLANDS AT THE WORLD CUP

• The Netherlands first appeared at the World Cup in 1934 in Italy, but were soon packing their bags after losing 3-2 to Switzerland in the first round. The Dutch fared no better four years later in France, going down 3-0 to Czechoslovakia after extra-time.

• **The Netherlands had to wait until 1974 before reaching the finals again, but they certainly made up for lost time. Inspired by their brilliant captain, the legendary Johan Cruyff, and playing a magical brand of free-flowing 'Total Football', the Dutch cruised through to the final where they faced hosts West Germany in Munich. Despite taking the lead in the first minute through a Johan Neeskens penalty, they were eventually beaten 2-1 in an epic contest.**

• Four years later the Dutch made it through to the final again, and once more they came up against the hosts – Argentina. Playing in front of a hostile home crowd, the Netherlands did well to take the game into extra-time but eventually went down 3-1. Nonetheless, the exciting football they produced at two World Cups earned them many admirers and the Dutch team of the 1970s is often rated the best of that decade.

• **After a 12-year gap, the Netherlands returned to the**

Frank Rijkaard's unseemly 'spat' with Rudi Voller in 1990

finals in 1990 with a team featuring stars like Marco van Basten, Ruud Gullit and Frank Rijkaard who had won the European Championships two years earlier. However, they were knocked out by old enemies Germany in a bad-tempered last 16 encounter.

• After losing to Brazil in the quarter-finals in 1994, the Netherlands again faced the South Americans four years later in France – this time at the semi-final stage. Agonisingly, the Dutch were defeated on penalties after a 1-1 draw and they then lost the third place play-off to surprise package Croatia.

• **Following a period in the doldrums in the early 2000s, the Dutch reached a third final in 2010 in South Africa. After beating Slovakia, Brazil and Uruguay in the knockout rounds, the Netherlands met European champions Spain in Johannesburg, in what many expected would be a feast of attacking football. However, the Dutch ruined the match as a spectacle by adopting an overly aggressive approach in an attempt to break up Spain's intricate passing game. Their brutal tactics almost worked, but a late Andres Iniesta goal consigned the Netherlands to a third defeat in the final.**

PREVIOUS TOURNAMENTS

1930 Did not enter	1966 Did not qualify	1994 Quarter-finals
1934 Round 1	1970 Did not qualify	1998 Fourth place
1938 Round 1	1974 Runners-up	2002 Did not qualify
1950 Did not enter	1978 Runners-up	2006 Round 2
1954 Did not enter	1982 Did not qualify	2010 Runners-up
1958 Did not qualify	1986 Did not qualify	
1962 Did not qualify	1990 Round 2	

CHILE

While Chile don't have a great World Cup record, the South Americans traditionally adopt a positive approach which can make them a tremendously exciting team to watch. The current Chilean side fall very much into that tradition, playing with a verve and panache that could take them far. Certainly, if they show the same form as they did while beating England 2-0 in a November 2013 friendly they could be serious dark horses this summer.

Chile's path to Brazil, though, was far from smooth. After three defeats on the trot their qualification hopes hung in the balance, but results picked up once Jorge Sampaoli took over as coach in December 2012. An Argentinian who previously managed a number of Chilean clubs, Sampaoli favours a dynamic, high-energy game which demands that his players attempt to win the ball back deep inside the opposition half.

These 'pressing' tactics helped Chile score 29 goals in qualification – a tally only bettered by group winners Argentina. Among the attacking players to impress during the campaign were Valencia striker Eduardo Vargas, Juventus midfielder Arturo Vidal and Barcelona's Alexis Sanchez, a genuinely world-class winger.

At the other end, though, Chile conceded 25 goals. No real blame could be laid at the door of Real Sociedad's Claudio Bravo, a capable goalkeeper who distributes the ball superbly, but the defence as a whole was unconvincing. The simple fact is that the full-backs – usually Mauricio Isla, of Juventus, and Nottingham Forest's Gonzalo Jara – are happier bombing up the pitch than protecting their own goal, while Gary Medel's lack of inches makes him suspect at centre-half. 'The Pitbull', as he's known, might be better employed in the midfield role he plays for Cardiff.

Still, for all these faults, Chile are a hugely entertaining side and will add much to the summer's Brazilian carnival.

> **"With these players, we can get enthusistic at the prospect that big things could happen."**
> Chile coach
> Jorge Sampaoli

CHILE AT THE WORLD CUP

• Chile's best performance at the World Cup was in 1962 when, as hosts, they reached the semi-finals. The Chileans' group game against Italy, though, was a grim affair, featuring two dismissals, a broken nose and numerous dangerous tackles in an encounter dubbed 'The Battle of Santiago'. Still, after beating the Italians 2-0, Chile marched on to the quarter-finals, where they defeated Russia before finally losing to Brazil in the last four.

• **Chile were thrown out of the 1990 World Cup when their goalkeeper feigned injury when a firecracker landed near him during a qualifier against Brazil. The referee believed that Rojas had been hurt and called the game off, but FIFA later awarded Brazil a 2-0 victory. As a further** punishment, Chile were banned altogether from the 1994 tournament in the USA.

• On their last appearance at the finals in 2010 Chile advanced from their group after beating both Honduras and Switzerland 1-0. In the last 16, however, the Chileans came up against in-form South American rivals Brazil and were trounced 3-0.

PREVIOUS TOURNAMENTS

1930 Round 1	1966 Round 1	1994 Banned
1934 Withdrew	1970 Did not qualify	1998 Round 2
1938 Withdrew	1974 Round 1	2002 Did not qualify
1950 Round 1	1978 Did not qualify	2006 Did not qualify
1954 Did not qualify	1982 Round 1	2010 Round 2
1958 Did not qualify	1986 Did not qualify	
1962 Third place	1990 Disqualified	

KEY PLAYER

ALEXIS SANCHEZ

If one player epitomises Chile's quicksilver passing style it is Barcelona's Alexis Sanchez, a fast, tricky winger who can torment any defence when he's on top form. For the past few years the 25-year-old has been a key man in the South Americans' attack, as he demonstrated to good effect when he scored both his team's goals in their surprise friendly win against England at Wembley in 2013.

After starting out with local side Cobreloa, Sanchez made his name with Italian club Udinese with whom he became the first Chilean player to score four goals in a Serie A fixture when he filled his boots in a 7-0 rout of Palermo in February 2011. Later that year he moved on to Barcelona in a £22 million deal, helping the Catalan giants win the Copa del Rey in his first season and La Liga in his second.

AUSTRALIA

Australia may have qualified for a third successive World Cup finals, but there is no doubting that the Socceroos are in a state of transition. Not only have they waved goodbye to some stalwarts of their 'Golden Generation', such as Chelsea's veteran reserve goalkeeper Mark Schwarzer, but they have also lost the coach who guided them to Brazil, Holger Osieck.

The German was given his marching orders after two consecutive 6-0 friendly defeats by Brazil and France. His replacement, Ange Postecoglou, may not be a household name, but he has an excellent record in Australian domestic football, leading South Melbourne to back-to-back titles and then on to the FIFA World Club Championship, and repeating that league success with Brisbane Roar.

In his first fixture in charge of the Aussies, a 1-0 friendly win over Costa Rica in November 2013, there were signs that the Greek-born coach was attempting to get his team to play more football from the back than his predecessor, while also demanding that his midfielders press high up the pitch in an effort to win the ball back quickly.

In terms of personnel, Postecoglou will probably choose his goalkeeper from Borussia Dortmund's Mitchell Langerak, Reading's Adam Federici or Bruges youngster Matthew Ryan. Otherwise, he will rely heavily on the old guard. Among the veterans to watch out for in Brazil are former Aston Villa midfielder Brett Holman, ex-Everton support striker Tim Cahill and bald-headed midfielder Mark Bresciano, formerly of Parma, Palermo and Lazio. Up front, Bayer Leverkusen striker Robbie Kruse will add some much-needed pace if he recovers from a knee injury in time, while Celtic starlet Tomas Rogic, now on loan at Melbourne Victory, could make an impact from the bench.

Whoever plays, though, few will expect Australia to progress from an extremely tough group.

> **"Nobody will give us much chance in this group and that's an opportunity in itself."**
> Australia coach
> Ange Postecoglou

AUSTRALIA AT THE WORLD CUP

• Australia made their World Cup debut in 1974 in West Germany, but returned to the southern hemisphere without managing a single goal in their three group games. The Socceroos, though, did at least claim a point from a battling 0-0 draw with Chile.

• Following a number of agonising near misses, the Aussies reached the finals again in 2006 in Germany. After opening with an excellent 3-1 win over Japan, Australia then lost to Brazil to leave them requiring a point from their last match with Croatia to advance to the knockout phase. That's precisely what they got, after a late Harry Kewell equaliser secured a famous 2-2 draw.

• Brilliantly organised by Dutch manager Guus Hiddink, the Socceroos made life difficult for eventual winners Italy in their last 16 encounter but were beaten by a highly controversial last-minute Francesco Totti penalty.

• The Aussies came close to repeating that achievement in 2010 in South Africa, but were pipped by Ghana to second place in their group on goal difference.

PREVIOUS TOURNAMENTS

1930 Did not enter	1966 Did not qualify	1994 Did not qualify
1934 Did not enter	1970 Did not qualify	1998 Did not qualify
1938 Did not enter	1974 Round 1	2002 Did not qualify
1950 Did not enter	1978 Did not qualify	2006 Round 2
1954 Did not enter	1982 Did not qualify	2010 Round 1
1958 Did not enter	1986 Did not qualify	
1962 Did not enter	1990 Did not qualify	

KEY PLAYER

MILE JEDINAK

A defensive midfielder who is known for his committed tackling, heading ability and inspirational leadership, Crystal Palace captain Mile Jedinak will hope to make more of an impression on this World Cup than the last one in South Africa, when his only appearance came in Australia's 4-0 drubbing by Germany in their opening fixture.

Certainly, if Jedinak reproduces his Palace form this summer then he will catch the eye. The curly-haired 29-year-old has been a pivotal figure at Selhurst Park since arriving from Turkish outfit Genclerbirligi in 2011, being voted Palace's 'Player of the Season' two years later after helping the Eagles gain promotion to the Premier League, thanks to a 1-0 play-off final win over Watford at Wembley.

First capped by his country in 2008 while he was still with Australian club Central Coast Mariners, Jedinak is now one of the most experienced players in the Aussies' squad and his know-how will be vital to a team which may struggle in a tough group in Brazil.

COLOMBIA

Over the years Colombia have provided some spectacular moments at the World Cup – think of Rene Higuita's eccentric goalkeeping and Carlos Valderrama's sublime skills (and crazy hair!) – without ever really achieving very much at the finals. The South Americans will hope to make a bigger impression this time round and after an excellent qualification campaign, which saw them finish second behind group winners Argentina, there is every reason for their fans to be optimistic.

Colombia's passage to Brazil was based on a sound defence, which conceded just 13 goals in their 16 qualifiers – the best record in the South American section. That's a stat which will have pleased the team's coach, the Argentinian Jose Pekerman, who is known for adopting an essentially cautious approach while also being fond of tactical experimentation.

> **"I think it will be a very even group and attractive thanks to the styles of the teams."**
> Colombia coach
> Jose Pekerman

Captain Mario Yepes of Italian side Atalanta is likely to be a key member of the Colombians' rearguard this summer, even though he will be 38 when the tournament kicks off. Ahead of him, Carlos 'The Rock' Sanchez of Elche will provide a solid barrier in midfield, allowing the creative talents of Monaco's James Rodriguez – a player once compared by Sir Alex Ferguson to Cristiano Ronaldo – to flourish in the final third.

With star striker Radamel Falcao likely to miss the finals after suffering a serious knee injury playing for club side Monaco in January, the goalscoring burden will instead fall on River Plate's Teofilo Gutierrez and Porto striker Jackson Martinez, who has been a transfer target for a number of leading Premier League clubs.

Colombia are one of the top eight seeds at the finals, but without the iconic Falcao they lack star quality and goalscoring potential. As a result, the South Americans may struggle to escape from what promises to be an extremely competitive and tightly-contested group.

COLOMBIA AT THE WORLD CUP

• Colombia first appeared at the World Cup in Chile in 1962. The South Americans picked up a point after coming from 4-1 down to draw 4-4 with Russia – equalling the highest-ever draw at the finals – but defeats against Uruguay (2-1) and Yugoslavia (5-0) ensured that they finished bottom of their group.

• **At Italia '90 Colombia made it into the second round for the first and only time to date, after finishing as one of the best third-placed sides. Sadly, a disastrous mistake by madcap goalkeeper Rene Higuita gifted veteran Cameroon striker Roger Milla the decisive goal in the teams' last 16 meeting.**

• Following a 5-0 victory away to Argentina in qualification, Colombia were tipped to do well at USA '94. However, they started badly with a 3-1 defeat to Romania and then lost 2-1 to the hosts, thanks in part to an own goal by Andres Escobar. Tragically, Escobar was shot dead by a group of irate Colombian fans shortly after he returned home.

PREVIOUS TOURNAMENTS

1930 Did not enter	1966 Did not qualify	1994 Round 1
1934 Did not enter	1970 Did not qualify	1998 Round 1
1938 Withdrew	1974 Did not qualify	2002 Did not qualify
1950 Withdrew	1978 Did not qualify	2006 Did not qualify
1954 Banned	1982 Did not qualify	2010 Did not qualify
1958 Did not qualify	1986 Did not qualify	
1962 Round 1	1990 Round 2	

KEY PLAYER

TEOFILO GUTIERREZ

A speedy striker who packs a powerful shot in his favourite right foot, Teofilo Gutierrrez will represent Colombia's main goal threat in Brazil in the likely absence of Radamel Falcao.

Born into desperate poverty in the slums of Barranquillo, Colombia's fourth biggest city, Gutierrez made his name with local side Atletico Junior, averaging a goal every other game before moving to Trabzonspor in 2010.

He failed to settle in Turkey, though, and the following year joined Racing Club of Argentina. The goals flowed again, but Gutierrez left under a cloud after a bizarre incident when he threatened a team-mate with a paintball gun. After that he had a brief spell with Mexican club Cruz Azul before returning to Argentina with River Plate in 2013.

Gutierrez was first capped by his country in 2009, scoring on his debut in a friendly against El Salvador. He performed impressively in the South American World Cup qualifiers, netting six goals to help Colombia book their spot in Brazil.

GREECE

Greece's qualification for the finals was a huge boost for a country which has suffered grave ecomonic problems since the financial crash of 2008. However, the Greeks put their supporters through the wringer along the way, narrowly missing out on an automatic slot on goal difference to Bosnia-Hercegovina before booking their place in Brazil with a hard-fought aggregate 4-2 victory over Romania in the play-offs.

Greece's success was built on a solid defence, which conceded just four goals in their 10 group games. Goalkeeper Orestis Karnezis of Granada, who played every minute of his team's qualifying campaign, kept eight clean sheets and was aided by an obdurate and tough-tackling back four, which was superbly marshalled by Borussia Dortmund centre-back Sokratis Papastathopoulos.

In midfield, Portuguese coach Fernando Santos relied heavily on two veterans of Greece's surprise triumph at Euro 2004: Kostas Katsouranis of PAOK and Fulham's Giorgos Karagounis, who is a renowned

> **"Our style of play generally remains the same. We are tough and we don't concede easily."**
> Greece captain
> Giorgos Karagounis

dead-ball specialist. However, with a combined age of more than 70 it's unlikely that both will start in the heat of Brazil, providing opportunities for younger players such as Olympiakos' Giannis Maniatis and the PAOK pair Alexandros Tziolis and Sotiris Ninis.

Up front, the lively Konstantinos Mitroglou was Greece's top scorer in qualification with five goals. He will probably be supported by the talented but unpredictable Celtic forward Giorgos Samaras and PAOK's Dimitris Salpingidis, another player well into his thirties. Both will be under strict instructions from Santos to drop into midfield when Greece lose possession, turning the team's 4-3-3 formation into an ultra-defensive 4-5-1.

A workmanlike side, Greece will make life tough for their opponents in Brazil but a lack of goals – they only managed 12 in their 10 group games – may ensure that their World Cup adventure is a short one.

GREECE AT THE WORLD CUP

• Surprisingly, Greece didn't play at the World Cup finals until 1994. The long wait to appear on the international stage had raised expectations in the country, but the Greeks' campaign proved to be nothing short of disastrous.

• Trounced 4-0 in their first match by Argentina, Greece then suffered another four-goal defeat to Bulgaria before losing 2-0 to Nigeria. With no points, no goals and 10 conceded Greece's terrible record was one of the worst in World Cup history.

• On their second appearance at the finals, in 2010 in South Africa, Greece did at last give their long-suffering fans something to cheer. A 2-0 defeat to South Korea represented a disappointing start but the Greeks then came from a goal down to beat Nigeria 2-1, Dimitris Salpingidis scoring his country's first goal at the tournament before Vasilios Torosidis gave Greece their first ever win.

• A 2-0 defeat to Argentina ended their hopes of progressing to the last 16, but at least Greece had done something to erase those painful and humiliating memories from USA '94.

PREVIOUS TOURNAMENTS

1930 Did not enter	1966 Did not qualify	1994 Round 1
1934 Withdrew	1970 Did not qualify	1998 Did not qualify
1938 Did not qualify	1974 Did not qualify	2002 Did not qualify
1950 Did not enter	1978 Did not qualify	2006 Did not qualify
1954 Did not qualify	1982 Did not qualify	2010 Round 1
1958 Did not qualify	1986 Did not qualify	
1962 Did not qualify	1990 Did not qualify	

KEY PLAYER

KONSTANTINOS MITROGLOU

Greece may not score many goals but in Konstantinos Mitroglou they have a player who can worry the very tightest of defences. What's more, the heavily-tattooed striker is in the form of his life and will go to Brazil bristling with confidence.

'Mitrogoal', as fans have dubbed him, was born in northern Greece but moved with his family at a young age to Germany. After learning his trade at Duisberg and Borussia Monchengladbach he made the move back to his homeland in 2007, when he joined Olympiakos.

In October 2013 Mitroglou made history when he became the first Greek player to score a Champions League hat-trick, in a 3-0 win at Anderlecht. The following month he became a hero to the whole Greek nation when he scored in both legs of his country's World Cup play-off.

In January 2014 Fulham broke their transfer record when they paid £11 million for Mitroglou.

IVORY COAST

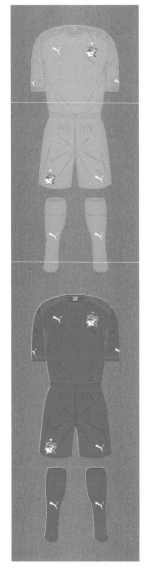

A team packed full of past and present Premier League players, Ivory Coast will be appearing at their third consecutive World Cup in Brazil this summer. In both 2006 and 2010 the Elephants were desperately unlucky in the draw, facing global heavyweights such as Argentina, the Netherlands, Brazil and Portugal in the group stages, but they have fared better this time round and will fancy their chances of progressing to the last 16 for the first time in their history.

Certainly, if the Africans show the same form as they did in qualifying then they should enjoy a decent tournament. After topping their initial group ahead of Morocco without losing a single game, Ivory Coast were then handed a tricky play-off against Senegal. After winning 3-1 in Abidjan, the Elephants secured their passage to Brazil with a 1-1 draw in the return leg, ex-Chelsea striker Salomon Kalou popping up with a vital late equaliser.

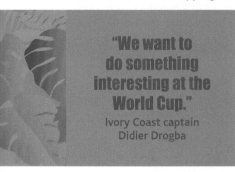

"We want to do something interesting at the World Cup."
Ivory Coast captain Didier Drogba

The Elephants' consistent form throughout the qualifying campaign will have delighted coach Sabri Lamouchi, a former French international midfielder appointed to the role in 2012. He has tried to instil a stronger team ethic in a side which previously had struggled to integrate fully some stunning individual talents into a cohesive unit.

Chief among the side's star names are former Chelsea legend Didier Drogba and Manchester City powerhouse Yaya Toure, African Player of the Year in 2011, 2012 and 2013. This stellar pair will be supported by the likes of the hard-working Kalou, Newcastle's industrious midfielder Cheick Tiote, dreadlocked ex-Arsenal striker Gervinho, veteran Liverpool defender Kolo Toure and Lokeren goalkeeper Boubacar Barry.

While it's true that these Elephants are a bit long in the tusk, the Ivory Coast are still a force to be reckoned with and they should have enough quality to reach the second round – where they could possibly face England in what would be a fascinating tie.

IVORY COAST AT THE WORLD CUP

• Ivory Coast first played at the World Cup in Germany in 2006. Drawn in the so-called 'Group of Death', the Elephants went down to a 2-1 defeat to Argentina in their opening match, legendary striker Didier Drogba grabbing the Ivory Coast's consolation goal.

• Another 2-1 defeat to the Netherlands followed, but the Africans avoided the wooden spoon by coming back from 2-0 down in their final match against Serbia & Montenegro to win 3-2 thanks to two goals from striker Aruna Dindane and a late penalty by substitute Bonaventure Kalou, brother of Salomon.

• Ivory Coast were unlucky to be paired in another tough group in 2010 in South Africa. An opening round 0-0 draw with Portugal represented a reasonable start, but after a 3-1 defeat to Brazil the Africans were playing catch-up. Needing a hatful of goals against minnows North Korea to have any chance of progressing to the knockout stages, they only managed a routine 3-0 win and had to be satisfied with third place in arguably the tournament's most difficult group.

PREVIOUS TOURNAMENTS

1930 Did not enter	1966 Did not enter	1994 Did not qualify
1934 Did not enter	1970 Did not enter	1998 Did not qualify
1938 Did not enter	1974 Did not qualify	2002 Did not qualify
1950 Did not enter	1978 Did not qualify	2006 Round 1
1954 Did not enter	1982 Did not enter	2010 Round 1
1958 Did not enter	1986 Did not qualify	
1962 Did not enter	1990 Did not qualify	

KEY PLAYER

DIDIER DROGBA

A talismanic figure for his country, Ivory Coast captain Didier Drogba is the Elephants' all-time leading scorer with more than 60 goals. And while now in the twilight of his glittering career, the powerfully-built Galatasaray striker is still a force to be reckoned with, a case in point being his third place in the 2013 African Player of the Year vote.

Winner of that Player of the Year award in 2006 and 2009, Drogba has twice reached the final of the African Nations Cup but both times finished on the losing side. However, his achievements with Chelsea, whom he joined from Marseille for £24 million in 2004, more than made up for those disappointments.

A three-time Premier League champion with the Blues, Drogba also won the FA Cup four times and thrived on the biggest stage, scoring in each of the four finals.

His greatest feat, though, came in his last game for the Londoners in 2012, when he scored a last-gasp equaliser in normal time, then slotted the winning penalty in the Champions League final shoot-out against Bayern Munich to cement his iconic status at Stamford Bridge.

JAPAN

Japan have become World Cup regulars since appearing in the finals for the first time in 1998, and in Brazil will be strutting their stuff on the global stage for the fifth tournament on the trot. While it's true that the Blue Samurai have never really grabbed the headlines, they have generally managed to give a good account of themselves and surpassed expectations last time round in South Africa by reaching the last 16.

For the third time in succession, Japan were the first country other than the hosts to qualify for the finals, thanks to a late penalty by Keisuke Honda which secured a 1-1 home draw against Australia. Since then, Japan have shown good form in a number of high-profile friendly matches, drawing 2-2 with the Netherlands and beating Belgium 3-2.

The signs, then, are encouraging for Japan boss Alberto Zaccheroni, an Italian who was formerly in charge of AC Milan, Inter and Juventus. His squad draws heavily on a number of experienced players who earn their trade in Europe, including defensive stalwarts Atsunto Uchida (Schalke) and Yuto Nagatomo (Inter).

However, it's in midfield where Japan's strength truly lies, with the likes of Honda, who signed for Italian giants AC Milan in January 2014, Manchester United's Shinji Kagawa and veteran skipper Yashito Endo all very capable on the ball.

Scoring goals has often been a problem for Japan at previous World Cups – indeed, they have averaged less than a goal a game in their 14 games at the finals – but they will boast a prolific striker in Mainz's Shinji Okazaki, the top scorer in the Asian qualifying section with eight goals.

If Okazaki brings his shooting boots to Brazil, Japan will add a dangerous cutting edge to their precise build-up play and could surprise many by progressing beyond the group stage.

> **"It's a shame to be drawn with the best African side."**
> Japan coach Alberto Zaccheroni clearly wanted to avoid Ivory Coast

JAPAN AT THE WORLD CUP

• Japan first competed at the World Cup in France in 1998 but they performed poorly, crashing to three straight defeats against Argentina, Croatia and Jamaica and only managing a single goal, scored by striker Masashi Nakayama.

• The Blue Samurai did better in 2002 when, as co-hosts with South Korea, they reached the last 16 after group-stage victories over both Russia (1-0) and Tunisia (2-0). However, a narrow 1-0 defeat to eventual semi-finalists Turkey in the first knockout round quickly shattered the national party mood.

• Japan disappointed at the 2006 finals in Germany, picking up just a single point from a 0-0 draw with Croatia while also suffering heavy defeats against Australia (3-1) and Brazil (4-1).

• On their last appearance at the finals, in 2010 in South Africa, Japan finished second in their group after beating both Cameroon (1-0) and Denmark (3-1). A last 16 clash with Paraguay appeared to open the path to a first quarter-final for Japan but, after a sleep-inducing 0-0 draw, the Asian side were knocked out on penalties, prompting the immediate resignation of coach Takeshi Okada.

PREVIOUS TOURNAMENTS

1930 Did not enter	1966 Did not qualify	1994 Did not qualify
1934 Did not enter	1970 Did not qualify	1998 Round 1
1938 Withdrew	1974 Did not qualify	2002 Round 2
1950 Banned	1978 Did not qualify	2006 Round 1
1954 Did not qualify	1982 Did not qualify	2010 Round 2
1958 Did not enter	1986 Did not qualify	
1962 Did not qualify	1990 Did not qualify	

KEY PLAYER

SHINJI KAGAWA

A wonderfully talented player who can operate effectively either on the wing or in midfield, Shinji Kagawa's vision, deft passing and goalscoring ability will be pivotal to Japan's hopes this summer.

Kagawa made his international debut against Ivory Coast in 2008, but was a surprise omission from his country's World Cup squad two years later. He did, though, help Japan win the Asian Cup in 2011, although he missed the final through injury.

After starting out with Cerezo Osaka in his homeland, Kagawa moved to Borussia Dortmund in 2010, and was an instrumental figure as the German giants won the league and cup Double two years later.

In the summer of 2012 he became the most expensive Asian player in Premier League history when he joined Manchester United for £17 million. He enjoyed a decent first season at Old Trafford, but since the arrival of new United manager David Moyes in the summer of 2013 his selection has not been guaranteed.

URUGUAY

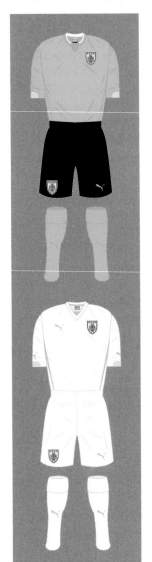

With a population of around 3.5 million, Uruguay will be the smallest country at this summer's World Cup. Mind you, the reigning Copa America champions are living proof that size doesn't matter, having won the tournament twice, in 1930 and 1950. More recently, the Uruguayans reached the semi-finals in South Africa in 2010 and with a star-studded attacking line-up they will have realistic hopes of doing at least as well in Brazil.

Sceptics, though, will point out that Uruguay struggled in qualification, finishing a poor fifth in the South American section and only booking their place at this summer's football festival after an emphatic play-off demolition of Jordan. The Uruguayans' problem throughout was a leaky defence, which conceded 25 goals in 16 group matches.

> **"This is the most difficult group, it will be the biggest challenge of our lives"**
> Uruguay captain
> Diego Lugano

Uruguay boss Oscar Tabarez, who has been in the job since 2006 and will be the longest-serving coach at the finals, will have to address that problem if his team are to progress from a tough group. It doesn't help, though, that his best defender is skipper Diego Lugano, a veteran who has barely played for his current club, West Brom.

At the other end of the pitch, however, Uruguay are a fearsome prospect. Liverpool's Luis Suarez, who was the top South American scorer in qualifying with 11 goals, and Paris Saint-Germain's Edinson Cavani are arguably the most potent strikeforce in the world. They could be joined by another famous name, former Manchester United forward Diego Forlan, if Tabarez opts to go for a 4-3-3 system rather than his usual 4-4-2 formation.

With the likes of Espanyol's Christian Stuani and Atletico Madrid's Christian Rodriguez supplying the ammunition for their stellar strikers, Uruguay may well be one of the most exciting teams for neutrals to watch this summer, but that suspect defence could scupper their hopes of recording a third World Cup triumph.

URUGUAY AT THE WORLD CUP

• In 1930 Uruguay became the first winners of the World Cup when they beat neighbours Argentina 4-2 in the final in Montevideo. A bizarre dispute about which ball to use was solved when the teams agreed to use an Argentinian ball in the first half and a Uruguayan one in the second half.

• **In 1950 Uruguay won the World Cup for a second time when they beat hosts Brazil 2-1 in the 'final' (it was actually the last match in a four-team final group). The match was witnessed by a crowd of 199,589 in the Maracana Stadium in Rio de Janeiro, the largest ever attendance at a football match.**

• Four years later Uruguay reached the semi-finals, before losing 4-2 to Hungary. The South Americans made the last four once again in Mexico in 1970, but were beaten 3-1 by Brazil.

• **Uruguay also reached the semi-finals in South Africa in 2010, following a controversial penalty shoot-out victory over Ghana in the quarter-finals. However, a 3-2 defeat to the Netherlands ended their hopes of playing in a third final.**

PREVIOUS TOURNAMENTS

1930 Winners	1966 Quarter-finals	1994 Did not qualify
1934 Withdrew	1970 Fourth place	1998 Did not qualify
1938 Did not enter	1974 Round 1	2002 Round 1
1950 Winners	1978 Did not qualify	2006 Did not qualify
1954 Fourth place	1982 Did not qualify	2010 Fourth place
1958 Did not qualify	1986 Round 2	
1962 Round 1	1990 Round 2	

KEY PLAYER

EDINSON CAVANI

Luis Suarez may be the most famous name in Uruguay's line-up but his strike partner Edinson Cavani will be just as vital to his country's chances this summer.

Now with Paris Saint-Germain, following a £55 million move from Napoli in 2013, Cavani possesses all the assets of a top-class centre-forward: pace, power, strength and the ability to finish accurately both on the ground and in the air.

Cavani scored against Colombia on his debut for Uruguay in 2008, and two years later helped his country reach the semi-finals of the World Cup in South Africa where they narrowly lost 3-2 to the Netherlands. In 2011 he was part of the Uruguayan side which beat Paraguay in the final of the Copa America.

He had to wait until the following year before winning his first domestic silverware, the Coppa Italia. The next season Cavani was top scorer in Serie A with 29 goals for Napoli, sparking a bidding war for his services among Europe's richest clubs.

COSTA RICA

Costa Rica will be playing at their fourth World Cup finals in Brazil – a remarkable achievement for such a small country. And while Los Ticos, as they are known to their fans, have never made a huge impact at the tournament, they have usually performed well. Given their excellent qualifying campaign, which saw them finish second in the final CONCACAF group behind the USA, there is no reason to suppose that this summer will be any different.

A sturdy rearguard was the key to Costa Rica's success in qualification, with Los Ticos only conceding a miserly seven goals in their 10 final pool games – the best record among the six teams. For a country which has historically put the onus on attack more than defence this impressive stat was a tribute to the sterling work of Colombian coach Jorge Luis Pinto, who has been in charge of the Costa Rica team since 2011.

> **"I believe in my team because we know how to act against the big teams."**
> Costa Rica coach
> Jorge Luis Pinto

Under Pinto, Los Ticos have reinvented themselves as an essentially defensive side, often employing three centre-backs in a bid to outnumber opposition attackers. Key members of this reinforced backline include Levante goalkeeper Keylor Navas and Mainz's Junior Diaz.

Further forward, Costa Rica look for inspiration from their captain, attacking midfielder Bryan Ruiz. A player with a deft touch who can dazzle when on song, Fulham star Ruiz, who was loaned out to PSV Eindhoven in the January 2014 transfer window, will hope to link up with young striker Joel Campbell, himself on loan at Greek side Olympiakos from Arsenal. Campbell is an exciting talent, but he will be watched carefully by referees after earning an official reprimand from FIFA for diving in a World Cup qualifier against the USA.

Costa Rica may be massive underdogs in a group with three previous tournament winners, but they are well-organised and could prove a tough nut to crack for their more illustrious opponents.

COSTA RICA AT THE WORLD CUP

• Competing for the first time at the World Cup in Italy in 1990, Costa Rica pulled off one of the greatest surprises in the tournament's history when they beat Scotland 1-0 in their opening fixture. Los Ticos then went down 1-0 to Brazil, before booking their place in the last 16 with a superb 2-1 victory over Sweden. However, a 4-1 defeat to Czechoslovakia saw them packing their bags for home.

• **Returning to the world stage in 2002, Costa Rica again performed admirably, defeating China 2-0 and drawing 1-1 with eventual semi-finalists Turkey in their opening two games. In their last group match, though, they came up against a rampant Brazil, and a 5-2 defeat meant they were pipped to second place by the Turks on goal difference.**

• Four years later, Costa Rica fared less well in Germany. Despite two goals from former Derby, West Ham and Manchester City striker Paulo Wanchope they went down 4-2 to the host nations in the tournament's opening fixture, and further defeats to Ecuador (3-0) and Poland (2-1) followed. That was Los Ticos' last appearance at the World Cup.

PREVIOUS TOURNAMENTS

1930 Did not enter	1966 Did not qualify	1994 Did not qualify
1934 Did not enter	1970 Did not qualify	1998 Did not qualify
1938 Did not enter	1974 Did not qualify	2002 Round 1
1950 Did not enter	1978 Did not qualify	2006 Round 1
1954 Did not enter	1982 Did not qualify	2010 Did not qualify
1958 Did not qualify	1986 Did not qualify	
1962 Did not qualify	1990 Round 2	

KEY PLAYER

BRYAN RUIZ

A tall, elegant attacking midfielder capable of producing moments of sublime skill, Bryan Ruiz is both Costa Rica's captain and the team's outstanding player. First capped by his country in 2005, he has now played more than 60 times for Los Ticos and was a pivotal figure in their qualification for the finals in Brazil.

After beginning his career with Costa Rican side Alajuelense, Ruiz forged his reputation with FC Twente. In a phenomenally successful debut season with the Dutch club in 2009/10, he helped them win the league title for the first time in their history and was his team's top scorer with 24 goals.

Ruiz joined Fulham for £10 million in August 2011 but divided opinion, with some deeming him an inconsistent 'luxury' player, while others arguing that he is a rare talent who deserves to be celebrated. The debate was put on hold in January 2014 when he joined PSV on loan.

ENGLAND

It's now nearly half a century since England captain Bobby Moore held aloft the World Cup trophy at Wembley in 1966, and not many people expect skipper Steven Gerrard to be doing the same in Brazil this summer. Still, the Three Lions will be desperate to make up for their wretchedly poor showing at the last finals in South Africa and some improved performances in the latter stages of the qualification campaign have created a sense of cautious optimism in the England camp.

2014 FIFA WORLD CUP BRAZIL™ QUALIFIERS
ENGLAND v POLAND
TUESDAY 15 OCTOBER 2013, WEMBLEY STADIUM
VAUXHALL

Indeed, boss Roy Hodgson will probably have images of those stirring victories over Montenegro and Poland racing through his mind as the weeks and days count down to the start of the tournament. His team played with a real sense of purpose in both games at Wembley, tigerishly hunting down the ball in the opposition half and then counter-attacking down the flanks at speed.

Hodgson will want to replicate the style of those performances in Brazil, but the climactic conditions – especially in England's first game in the Amazon rainforest against Italy – will not favour a high-tempo approach. If they are to prosper, England will need to keep possession better than they have done at previous World Cups.

Hodgson has players who can do that – the likes of Gerrard, Manchester United's Michael Carrick and star man Wayne Rooney – but he will also want to push opponents onto the back foot with the sheer pace of young Tottenham winger Andros Townsend and clever Liverpool striker Daniel Sturridge.

If the coach decides to be bolder still, there may even be a starting place for either Everton's Ross Barkley or Southampton's Adam Lallana, two exciting attacking midfielders who have quickly come to the fore.

Hodgson's first concern, though, will simply be to get through a very tough group where they must get the better of two other former World Cup winners. After that, anything is possible.

> "It's a tough group, no doubt about that. With Uruguay and Italy we've almost got two number one seeds."
>
> England coach
> Roy Hodgson

THE GAFFER: ROY HODGSON

One of the most experienced coaches in the game, Roy Hodgson has managed four Premier League clubs, four different national teams and club sides in five countries apart from England.

Hodgson's Three Lions' reign began reasonably well, as he led them to the quarter-finals of Euro 2012, where his team lost on penalties to Italy. He then guided England through the qualification campaign for Brazil, with his side remaining unbeaten in their 10 games.

After failing to make the grade as a player with Crystal Palace, Hodgson spent much of his early career in Sweden, winning the league with Halmstad in 1979 and then leading Malmo to five consecutive titles between 1985 and 1989. His other major successes include taking Switzerland to the World Cup in 1994, reaching the UEFA Cup final with Inter Milan in 1997 and, perhaps most impressively, steering unfashionable Fulham to the inaugural Europa League final in 2010.

After a short and unhappy spell with Liverpool in 2010/11, Hodgson got back on track with West Bromwich Albion before getting the nod from the Football Association in May 2012. At 64, he was the oldest man ever to be appointed England manager.

KEY PLAYER

WAYNE ROONEY

The most gifted England player of his generation, Wayne Rooney will be especially keen to shine in Brazil as he has had a pretty miserable time at his two previous World Cups.

In Germany in 2006 Rooney's often volatile temperament was exposed when he stamped on Portugal's Ricardo Carvalho in the quarter-final, earning a red card which ultimately cost his team dear. Four years later in South Africa, he was a pale shadow of his normal self as England limped out in the last 16 after being thrashed by Germany.

Rooney, then, has a definite point to prove this summer. If he wants to be classed with the elite names of world football he needs to show much more of the sometimes spectacular form that has made him one of England's highest goalscorers of all time, and won him a host of honours with Manchester United – including five Premier League titles and the Champions League in 2008.

He has the talent, but will he deliver on the biggest stage of all? Over to you, Roo.

ONE TO WATCH: ANDROS TOWNSEND

Fleet-footed Tottenham winger Andros Townsend became an overnight sensation when he performed brilliantly on his England debut in a World Cup qualifier against Montenegro at Wembley in October 2013, capping his impressive display with a spectacular strike from the edge of the box.

It's been a remarkable turnaround in fortune for the 22-year-old from east London, as for a number of years his career appeared to be drifting rather aimlessly. After struggling to get into the Tottenham first team, Townsend was loaned out to no fewer than eight clubs in the lower leagues, including Ipswich, Birmingham and Leeds United, before finally making his mark in the Premier League on loan at QPR in the 2012/13 season.

He returned to White Hart Lane for the start of the following campaign, and immediately caught England manager Roy Hodgson's eye with his direct attacking play down the flanks and ability to cut inside to take a shot at goal.

Just days after his stunning international debut, Townsend played equally well in a 2-0 win over Poland. Still a bit of an unknown quantity, he could be Hodgson's wild card in Brazil.

TACTICS BOARD
WAYNE'S WORLD

Formerly very much a 4-4-2 man, Roy Hodgson has now embraced a more modern 4-2-3-1 system that makes good use of his pacy widemen and his star player, Wayne Rooney.

If Rooney gets a lot of the ball in his position just behind Daniel Sturridge, the likely central striker, then various possibilities open up for the team. From his slightly withdrawn position, Rooney can try to feed Sturridge or spread play out to the wingers, probably the speedy Andros Townsend on the right and the hard-working Danny Welbeck on the left, or even try for goal himself.

Behind this front four, skipper Steven Gerrard will attempt to catch opposition defences out with his trademark long diagonals from deep, while alongside him either Michael Carrick or Frank Lampard keep play ticking over with shorter passes.

Additional width comes from the full-backs, Glen Johnson and – most likely – Leighton Baines, who is a particularly fine crosser from the left.

ENGLAND AT THE WORLD CUP

• Along with the other home countries, England declined to enter the World Cup in the 1930s following a dispute with FIFA about payments to amateur players. When England did finally make their debut in Brazil in 1950 they crashed out of the group stage after a shock 1-0 defeat to the USA – one of the biggest surprises in the tournament's history.

• After reaching the quarter-finals in 1954 and 1962, England won the tournament on home soil in 1966. Geoff Hurst scored a hat-trick in the 4-2 defeat of West Germany in the final, including a highly controversial second in extra-time when his shot bounced down off the crossbar and onto or – as England fans always insist – just over the line. To the delight of the home fans, the referee gave the goal after consulting with one of his assistants.

• England's defence of their trophy four years later got off to a nightmare start when, en route to Mexico, skipper Bobby Moore was arrested in Colombia on suspicion of stealing an expensive bracelet from a shop. He was eventually released to help England reach the quarter-finals, where they lost 3-2 to old rivals West Germany after extra-time.

• After failing to qualify for the finals in 1974 and 1978, England

Geoff Hurst scores his controversial second goal in 1966

reached the second stage in Spain in 1982 but were knocked out despite not losing one of their five games.

• England striker Gary Lineker's six goals at the 1986 tournament won him the Golden Boot, but Bobby Robson's team were eliminated in the quarter-finals by Argentina, thanks partly to the infamous 'Hand of God' goal by the South Americans' captain, Diego Maradona.

• England had another dose of bad luck at the 1990 finals in Italy, going out on penalties to West Germany in the semi-finals. The Three Lions have since endured

more shoot-out agony against Argentina in the last 16 in 1998, and against Portugal in the quarter-finals in 2006. In between, Sven Goran Eriksson's side were beaten 2-1 by eventual winners Brazil in the 2002 quarter-finals.

• Fabio Capello's England side performed poorly at the last finals in South Africa in 2010, only just making it out of the group stage and then losing 4-1 to Germany in the last 16. It might have been different, though, if the officials hadn't ruled out a clear Frank Lampard 'goal' when his shot bounced down off the crossbar and well over the line.

PREVIOUS TOURNAMENTS

1930 Did not enter	1966 Winners	1994 Did not qualify
1934 Did not enter	1970 Quarter-finals	1998 Round 2
1938 Did not enter	1974 Did not qualify	2002 Quarter-finals
1950 Round 1	1978 Did not qualify	2006 Quarter-finals
1954 Quarter-finals	1982 Round 2	2010 Round 2
1958 Round 1	1986 Quarter-finals	
1962 Quarter-finals	1990 Fourth place	

ITALY

With four World Cup triumphs in their locker – the last in 2006 – Italy are the most successful European country of all time at the finals. However, glorious images of those historic triumphs faded somewhat at the last tournament in South Africa when the Azzurri finished bottom of their group – even behind minnows New Zealand. To put it bluntly, the pressure will be on Italy to perform much, much better this time round.

Although their side has not changed a great deal since four years ago, the Italians have reason to be confident in Brazil. Since that appalling campaign of 2010 they have shown their true class by reaching the final of Euro 2012 – beating both England and Germany along the way – and qualifying for this summer's finals without losing a single match.

> **"We're going to have to sweat it out. They're going to be some very interesting matches."**
> Italy coach Cesare Prandelli

Much of the credit for this renaissance should go to Italy coach Cesare Prandelli, who has gradually introduced younger players, such as AC Milan winger Stephan El Shaarawy and Paris Saint-Germain midfielder Marco Verratti, without jettisoning a whole generation of players who have served the Azzurri well in the past.

Prandelli's 'evolution not revolution' approach means there will be many familiar faces in the Italian side, including veteran goalkeeper Gianluigi Buffon, old-stager Juventus defenders Giorgio Chiellini and Andrea Barzagli, brilliant deep-set playmaker Andrea Pirlo and attacking midfielder Riccardo Montolivo.

However, when the Italians stride out for their first match against England there's no doubt that all eyes will be focused on Mario Balotelli, the unpredictable and enigmatic former Manchester City striker, now with AC Milan. How he plays in Brazil will have a huge bearing on how far Italy progress which, given the completely off-the-wall nature of Balotelli's temperament, means that all predictions are pretty much worthless.

THE GAFFER: CESARE PRANDELLI

After a shocking 2010 World Cup in South Africa, Italy turned to Cesare Prandelli as the man to restore national pride and the former Fiorentina manager has done an excellent job.

On taking over the reins Prandelli said, "My intention is to work, work, work and I sincerely believe in rebuilding." He has been true to his word, introducing a batch of new players alongside grizzled veterans like Andrea Pirlo and Gianluigi Buffon and vastly improving Italy's fortunes along the way. To the surprise of many, the Italians reached the final of Euro 2012 and, although they were soundly beaten by Spain, they showed enough at the tournament to suggest that Prandelli had transformed morale in a previously demotivated squad.

The 56-year-old then continued his good work, by guiding his country through qualification for Brazil without losing a single match.

A midfielder with Atalanta and Juventus in his playing days, Prandelli managed five other Italian clubs, including Roma and Parma, before becoming Fiorentina boss in 2005. He led the Florence team to the semi-finals of the UEFA Cup in 2008, where they lost on penalties to Rangers, and the last 16 of the Champions League two years later.

KEY PLAYER

MARIO BALOTELLI

Love him or loathe him, you just can't ignore Mario Balotelli. The AC Milan striker is a genuine maverick, capable of leaving an indelible impression on a match with a piece of stunning brilliance or an act of gross stupidity.

Balotelli, though, has generally been on his best behaviour when wearing the blue shirt of Italy. At Euro 2012, for instance, he was in superb form, most notably in the semi-final against Germany when he scored twice in a surprise 2-1 win. In the World Cup qualifiers, too, he performed well, top-scoring for Italy with four goals, although he blotted his copybook by punching a wall in frustration after being sent off against the Czech Republic.

Headline-grabbing incidents like that were commonplace throughout his two-year spell at Manchester City, during which he helped the club win both the FA Cup and the Premier League but also turned then-manager Roberto Mancini's hair grey with a series of madcap antics, training ground bust-ups and on-field strops.

'Super Mario' or 'Barmy Balotelli'? The world awaits to see which one turns up in Brazil.

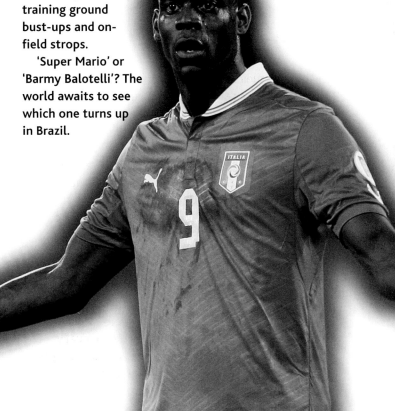

ONE TO WATCH: STEPHAN EL SHAARAWY

One of the most highly rated young players in European football, AC Milan winger Stephan El Shaarawy is a superb dribbler of the ball who has been compared to Barcelona icons Neymar and Lionel Messi.

He may not quite have hit those heights as yet, but the 21-year-old has shown enough in his short career to date to suggest he could soon rival those stellar names. 'The Pharoah', as he's been dubbed for his part-Egyptian heritage, started out with Genoa, becoming the fourth youngest ever Serie A player when he made his debut for the club aged 16 and 55 days. He rose to prominence, though, on loan at Padova in 2010/11, where he won the Serie B Player of the Year award after a series of dazzling displays. A move to Italian giants AC Milan followed, and in October 2012 he became their youngest ever scorer in the Champions League when he found the net against Zenit Saint Petersburg.

Long identified as a star of the future, El Shaarawy came through the various Italian national youth teams to make his senior debut in a friendly against England in August 2012.

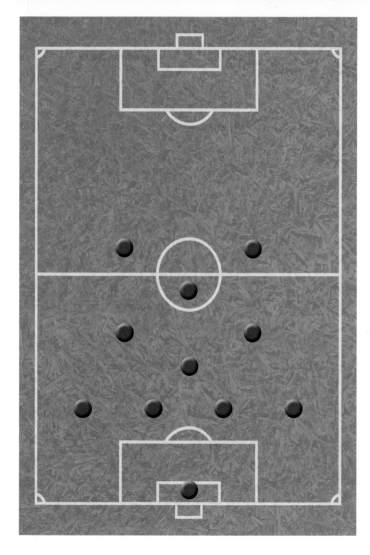

TACTICS BOARD

PIRLO THE PLAYMAKER

For many years Juventus midfielder Andrea Pirlo has been Italy's most important player, creating countless chances for his team with his pinpoint passing and ability to spot an opening.

That remains the case although, now in his mid-thirties, there are doubts over whether Pirlo will last 90 minutes in the heat of Brazil. Italy coach Cesare Prandelli, then, will be concerned to give his veteran deep-lying playmaker plenty of support in defensive situations, and will instruct the two wide men in his diamond midfield, Roma's Daniele de Rossi and Juventus' Claudio Marchisio, to close down spaces quickly when Italy lose possession.

Ahead of them, Milan's Riccardo Montolivo is the main link to the two strikers, his team-mate Mario Balotelli and pony-tailed hitman Pablo Osvaldo. Alternatively, Prandelli could opt for a 4-3-3 with possible places for two wingers, Milan's fleet-footed Stephan El Shaarawy and Sunderland's hard-working Emanuele Giaccherini, either side of Balotelli.

ITALY AT THE WORLD CUP

• Italy won the World Cup at the first attempt as hosts in 1934, thanks to a 2-1 win over Czechoslovakia in the final in Rome. In a bizarre postscript, Raimondo Orsi tried to recreate his viciously swerving equalising goal the next day for the benefit of photographers, but failed 20 times even without a goalkeeper between the posts!

• **Four years later Italy retained the trophy after beating Hungary 4-2 in the final in Paris. The intervention of World War II meant that the Italians held the trophy until 1950 – a record 16 years in total.**

• The Italians suffered arguably the greatest ever upset in World Cup history when they were beaten 1-0 in the group stage by minnows North Korea in 1966. Returning home early from England, the Italy squad was pelted with rotten tomatoes by hundreds of angry fans at Genoa Airport.

• **Four years later, though, Italy reached the final again in Mexico. Although they were hammered 4-1 by a brilliant Brazil side, the Italians could claim to have won the most exciting game of the finals – a thrilling 4-3 triumph over West Germany in the semi-finals.**

Italian delight and West German woe after the 1982 World Cup final

• Italy won the tournament for a third time in Spain in 1982, despite limping through the group stage with three unimpressive draws against Cameroon, Peru and Poland. That poor early form was forgotten, though, when the Italians beat West Germany 3-1 in the final in Madrid.

• **Italy hosted the tournament for a second time in 1990 but finished third after a semi-final defeat to Argentina. There was some consolation, though, for Italian striker Toto Schillaci, whose six goals in the tournament won him the Golden Boot.**

• Four years later Italy reached the final in the USA, but lost on penalties to Brazil. Three Italians missed from the spot, including star striker Roberto Baggio who blazed his kick high over the bar to hand the trophy to the South Americans.

• **Italy became the first European country to win the World Cup four times when they beat France on penalties in the final in Germany in 2006. Defender Fabio Grosso calmly put away the decisive spot-kick to give his side a 5-3 victory in the shoot-out after a tense 1-1 draw.**

• Four years later, Italy defended their trophy in dismal fashion in South Africa. After drawing with Paraguay and rank outsiders New Zealand, the Italians then lost 3-2 to Slovakia to finish bottom of their group.

PREVIOUS TOURNAMENTS

1930 Did not enter	1966 Round 1	1994 Runners-up
1934 Winners	1970 Runners-up	1998 Quarter-finals
1938 Winners	1974 Round 1	2002 Round 2
1950 Round 1	1978 Fourth place	2006 Winners
1954 Round 1	1982 Winners	2010 Round 1
1958 Did not qualify	1986 Round 2	
1962 Round 1	1990 Third place	

SWITZERLAND

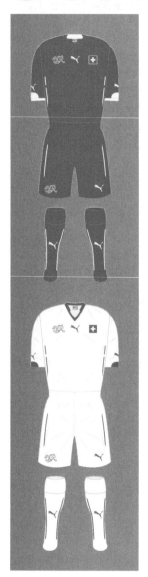

At the last World Cup Switzerland famously beat eventual winners Spain in their opening match, but still failed to get out of their group after two disappointing later results. It is precisely that sort of inconsistency that long-serving manager Ottmar Hitzfeld, in place since 2008, has attempted to remedy in recent years and, judging by his side's unbeaten qualifying campaign, he is doing a pretty good job.

The Swiss, though, were fortunate in being drawn in the least demanding of European groups, along with Iceland, Norway, Slovenia, Albania and Cyprus.

"France are the favourites. We hope to make the last 16 with them."
Switzerland coach Ottmar Hitzfeld

Still, you can only beat what's in front of you and Switzerland certainly did that, finishing an impressive seven points clear of the field. Indeed, so good was their form that, to the surprise of virtually everyone, FIFA awarded the Swiss a top-seed ranking at this summer's finals.

A canny operator who was previously in charge of Bayern Munich and Borussia Dortmund, Hitzfeld will not be carried away by his side's new official status. He will know, for instance, that the Swiss lack a top-class striker to make the best use of the chances created by fine midfielders such as Bayern's Xherdan Shaqiri, Borussia Monchengladbach's Granit Xhaka – a player Hitzfeld has dubbed 'a young Schweinsteiger' for his boundless energy – and the Napoli pair of skipper Gokhan Inler and Valon Behrami, formerly of West Ham.

The fact that Basel centre-back Fabian Schar was Switzerland's top scorer in qualifying tells its own story. However, the Swiss are adept at sharing out the goals and they have a resolute defence – which leaked only six goals in qualification – in front of goalkeeper Diego Benaglio, a Bundesliga title winner with Wolfsburg in 2009.

All in all they have a decent team, and while they may not live up to their starry FIFA ranking they won't embarrass themselves either.

SWITZERLAND AT THE WORLD CUP

• Switzerland have reached the quarter-finals of the World Cup on three occasions, most recently as hosts in 1954 when they were beaten 7-5 by Austria in the highest-scoring ever match at the tournament finals.

• **Following a 28-year absence from the world stage Switzerland qualified for USA '94 under their English coach, Roy Hodgson. They** did pretty well, too, reaching the second round before losing 3-0 to Spain.

• In 2006 Switzerland became the first ever team to be knocked out of the World Cup without conceding a single goal. Following a 0-0 draw with France, the Swiss then beat both Togo and South Korea 2-0 to advance to the second round. Their defence held firm again in the last 16 against Ukraine but after a 0-0 draw the Swiss lost in the penalty shoot-out.

• **At their last appearance in the finals in 2010 the Swiss pulled off a major surprise when they beat Spain 1-0 in their opening match. However, after losing to Chile and drawing with Honduras, the Swiss could only finish third in their group.**

PREVIOUS TOURNAMENTS

1930 Did not enter	1966 Round 1	1994 Round 2
1934 Quarter-finals	1970 Did not qualify	1998 Did not qualify
1938 Quarter-finals	1974 Did not qualify	2002 Did not qualify
1950 Round 1	1978 Did not qualify	2006 Round 2
1954 Quarter-finals	1982 Did not qualify	2010 Round 1
1958 Did not qualify	1986 Did not qualify	
1962 Round 1	1990 Round 2	

KEY PLAYER

XHERDAN SHAQIRI

A creative midfielder who boasts excellent close control, Bayern Munich's Xherdan Shaqiri provides a touch of flair in an otherwise rather pragmatic Swiss side.

Born in Kosovo in 1991, Shaqiri moved to Switzerland with his ethnic Albanian parents the following year as war engulfed their homeland. On the books of Basel from an early age, Shaqiri made his first-team debut as a 17-year-old and went on to win three league titles with the Swiss giants before joining Bayern in the summer of 2012.

His first season with the Bavarians was hugely successful, as Bayern won an unforgettable treble – the Bundesliga title, the German Cup and the Champions League – although Shaqiri didn't get off the bench in the final against Borussia Dortmund at Wembley.

Swiss Player of the Year in 2011 and 2012, Shaqiri made his international debut in 2010, scoring his first goal for his country with a brilliant 30-yarder against England in a Euro 2012 qualifier.

ECUADOR

After failing to make it to South Africa four years ago, Ecuador will be delighted to appear on the world stage for a third time this millennium. The South Americans qualified automatically for Brazil but it was a close run thing, as they just pipped Uruguay to fourth spot in their group on goal difference and so avoided a play-off for the last available World Cup place.

Ecuador's successful campaign was founded on their strong home form. Taking advantage of the high altitude in the capital Quito, which stands 2,800 metres above sea level, they were unbeaten at home in all nine games – just as well, really, as they failed to win a single away match. The Ecuadorians' penultimate fixture with Uruguay was key, the home side winning 1-0 which virtually guaranteed their qualification.

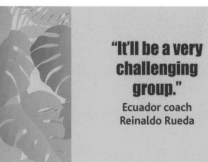

> "It'll be a very challenging group."
>
> Ecuador coach
> Reinaldo Rueda

An athletic, pacy and physically strong side, Ecuador are managed by Reinaldo Rueda, a Colombian who took Honduras to the last World Cup. He has introduced a direct, hard-running style with an emphasis on getting crosses into the box for burly lone striker Felipe Caicedo, a flop at Manchester City a few years back but Ecuador's top scorer in qualification with seven goals.

It is a system which demands good service from the wings and Ecuador are fortunate in having two excellent wide men in the form of Manchester United's Antonio Valencia and the speedy Jefferson Montero, scorer of that vital goal against the Uruguayans. Otherwise, there is not much flair in what is essentially a pragmatic, functional side in which former Everton loanee Segundo Castillo plays a pivotal role, patrolling the area in front of a robust and combative back four.

Ecuador are probably the weakest of the South American sides at the finals, but the draw has been relatively kind to them and they will hope to progress beyond the group stage.

ECUADOR AT THE WORLD CUP

• After years of trying, Ecuador finally made it to the World Cup finals in 2002 in Japan and South Korea. Following defeats against Italy and Mexico, the South Americans bounced back to beat Croatia 1-0 in their last game but it wasn't enough to prevent them finishing bottom of their group.

• The Ecuadorians fared better on their only other World Cup

appearance, in Germany in 2006. **After a surprise 2-0 win over Poland, Ecuador booked their place in the second round with an emphatic 3-0 victory against Costa Rica before going down 3-0 to the hosts in their final group game.**

• In the last 16, Ecuador were paired with England and gave Sven Goran Eriksson's men an early scare when

Carlos Tenorio's shot deflected off Ashley Cole and onto the bar. However, the South Americans' brave resistance was eventually ended by England skipper David Beckham, who curled a trademark free-kick into the net on the hour for the only goal of the game.

• Ecuador's Ivan Hurtado played in a record 68 World Cup qualifiers between 1994 and 2010.

PREVIOUS TOURNAMENTS

1930 Did not enter	1966 Did not qualify	1994 Did not qualify
1934 Did not enter	1970 Did not qualify	1998 Did not qualify
1938 Did not enter	1974 Did not qualify	2002 Round 1
1950 Withdrew	1978 Did not qualify	2006 Round 2
1954 Did not enter	1982 Did not qualify	2010 Did not qualify
1958 Did not enter	1986 Did not qualify	
1962 Did not qualify	1990 Did not qualify	

KEY PLAYER

ANTONIO VALENCIA

A player very much in the mould of the Ecuador team as a whole, Antonio Valencia is a direct winger who relies more on pace, strength and stamina than tricky skills when he takes on defenders.

Nonetheless, he is a highly effective performer who can make life extremely awkward for his marker.

Valencia first played for Ecuador in 2005, scoring twice in a 5-2 victory against Paraguay. The following year he played in all four of his country's games at the World Cup in Germany as Ecuador advanced to the second round where they were knocked out 1-0 by England. He has now won over 70 caps.

After starting out with Quito-based club El Nacional, Valencia joined La Liga outfit Villarreal in 2005 but was quickly loaned out to Recreativo. In 2006 he moved to Wigan Athletic, initially on loan, where his hard-running style soon won admirers and attracted the attention of the bigger clubs.

Three years later he joined Manchester United for around £16 million and has since won two league titles with the Old Trafford outfit.

FRANCE

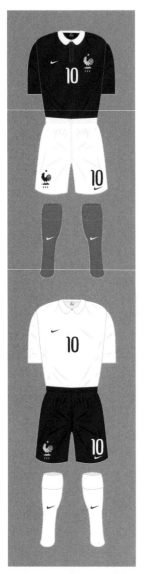

France's last World Cup campaign in South Africa was so shambolic it was later the subject of a government enquiry. Their supporters will be hoping that their heroes put on a better show in Brazil this summer and the signs are promising: on paper at least, France have a team that can rival just about any at the finals and they have also had the good fortune of being drawn in an eminently winnable group.

Less positively, the French made hard work of qualifying for Brazil. Finishing second in their group behind holders Spain was no disgrace, but Les Bleus then got into real difficulties in their play-off against Ukraine. Staring into the abyss after a 2-0 defeat in the first leg in Kiev, Didier Deschamps' team needed to pull out the stops in the second leg in Paris.

> "When you start a competition, the most important thing is to win the first match."
>
> France coach Didier Deschamps

France rose to the occasion, however, as two goals from Liverpool defender Mamadou Sakho and one from Real Madrid striker Karim Benzema secured a 3-0 win.

Along with Benzema, France's main goal threat comes from Bayern Munich winger Franck Ribery, who was his country's top scorer in qualification with five goals. In midfield, Deschamps has no shortage of players to pick from, with the likes of Paris Saint-Germain's Yohan Cabaye, Manchester City's Samir Nasri and former Manchester United youngster Paul Pogba among those hoping for a starting place.

There's every chance, meanwhile, that France's back five will be made up entirely of Premier League players, with Patrice Evra (Manchester United), Laurent Koscielny (Arsenal), Mathieu Debuchy (Newcastle) and Sakho figuring ahead of Tottenham's excellent shot-stopper Hugo Lloris.

France undoubtedly have the talent to progress far at the finals but, as one of the most unpredictable and enigmatic football nations on the planet, only a brave man would put money on it.

THE GAFFER: DIDIER DESCHAMPS

Appointed manager of Les Bleus in July 2012 as successor to Laurent Blanc, Didier Deschamps is a legendary figure in French football.

In a glorious playing career, he skippered France to triumph in the World Cup on home soil in 1998 and two years later led his side to victory in the European Championships. He retired from international football after that second success, having accumulated 103 caps – a record for France at the time, although his tally has since been surpassed by a number of players, including his former team-mates Marcel Desailly, Thierry Henry and Patrick Vieira.

A ball-playing defensive midfielder who was once famously described as a mere 'water carrier' by maverick French striker Eric Cantona, Deschamps also won an armful of silverware with his club teams, including the Champions League with both Marseille and Juventus, and the FA Cup with Chelsea during a season-long stint with the Londoners in 1999/2000.

After hanging up his boots Deschamps moved into management, first with Monaco, who he led to the Champions League final in 2004. After a short spell with Juventus, he returned to France with Marseille, guiding them to a first French league title for 18 years in 2010.

KEY PLAYER

KARIM BENZEMA

After surprisingly missing out on the last World Cup in South Africa, Real Madrid striker Karim Benzema will be desperate to do well at this year's finals.

The 26-year-old certainly has everything in his locker to be a major star at the tournament. A strong and powerful runner who can shoot with either foot and also poses a threat in the air, Benzema has the ability to frighten any defence.

He initially rose to prominence with his hometown club, Lyon, enjoying a superb season in 2008/09 when he was voted Ligue 1 Player of the Year. A £30 million move to Madrid followed, but Benzema struggled to settle in the Spanish capital at first, gaining weight and famously being described as 'listless' by then manager Jose Mourinho. His form picked up, though, and during the 2011/12 season he became the highest ever French scorer in La Liga, passing the previous best of the legendary Zinedine Zidane.

Restored to the France national team, Benzema led the line for his country at Euro 2012 and will do the same again in Brazil.

ONE TO WATCH: PAUL POGBA

A tall, powerful midfielder whose surging runs from deep have seen him compared to France and Arsenal legend Patrick Vieira, Juventus' Paul Pogba is tipped by many to make a huge impact at this summer's World Cup.

He has already made a mark at international level, performing superbly as Les Bleus came from 2-0 down in the first leg of their play-off against Ukraine to book their place in Brazil with a 3-0 victory in the return in Paris. Considering that he had only made his debut for France six months earlier, Pogba's selection by coach Didier Deschamps in such a vital match was a clear indication of how highly he is rated.

Winner of the 2013 Golden Boy award for the best Under-21 player in Europe, Pogba started out with Le Havre before moving to Manchester United in 2009 aged just 16. He made a handful of first-team appearances for the Old Trafford outfit in the 2011/12 season, but at the end of the campaign moved on to Juventus. Nicknamed 'Paul the Octopus' in Italy for his tentacle-like long legs, he helped Juve win the league in his first year in Turin.

TACTICS BOARD
FEEDING FRANCK

France coach Didier Deschamps fielded two strikers, Karim Benzema and Olivier Giroud, in a number of qualifiers but he is likely to leave the Arsenal man on the bench in Brazil and send his team out in a 4-3-3 formation.

Much of France's threat comes down the left, where Bayern Munich's brilliant wide man Franck Ribery operates, sometimes in tandem with overlapping full-back Patrice Evra. The hard-working midfield trio of Paris Saint-Germain pair Yohan Cabaye and Blaise Matuidi and Juventus starlet Paul Pogba will look to feed Ribery as often as possible, although not to the extent of neglecting Marseille's Mathieu Valbuena, another skilful and creative player, on the right-hand side of the attack.

In defence, goalkeeper Hugo Lloris has a high starting position and moves incredibly quickly to snuff out danger, acting almost as a sweeper just behind the two regular centre-backs, Arsenal's Laurent Koscielny and Liverpool's Mamadou Sakho.

FRANCE AT THE WORLD CUP

• France played in the first ever World Cup match, thrashing Mexico 4-1 in Montevideo, Uruguay on 13 July 1930. In front of a paltry crowd of just 3,000 in the Pocitos stadium, France's Lucien Laurent wrote himself into World Cup history by scoring the tournament's first ever goal after 19 minutes.

• **France hosted the tournament for the first time in 1938, and the hosts got off to a dream start when they scored after just 40 seconds in the first round against neighbours Belgium. In the quarter-finals, though, they came up against the holders Italy and went down to a 3-1 defeat.**

Harald Schumacher misses the ball but not Patrick Battiston in 1982

• In Sweden in 1958 France fared better, finishing in third place after losing 5-2 to eventual champions Brazil in the semi-finals. French striker Just Fontaine set a still unbeaten record for the tournament by scoring 13 goals, including three against Paraguay and four in the play-off for third place against West Germany.

• **In 1982 France reached the semi-finals again, but lost in the first ever World Cup penalty shoot-out against West Germany. The game, though, is best remembered for a violent challenge by German goalkeeper Harald Schumacher on Patrick Battiston, which knocked out three of the Frenchman's teeth and left him unconscious. Incredibly, the referee didn't even award France a free-kick.**

• After a third semi-final defeat in 1986, France finally reached the final on home soil in 1998. Their opponents, reigning champions Brazil, were beaten surprisingly easily, star player Zinedine Zidane scoring twice and Arsenal midfielder Emmanuel Petit adding a third as France won 3-0. More than a million people celebrated their country's triumph in the streets of Paris.

• **Four years later France put up an unexpectedly weak defence of their trophy, going out in the group phase after shock defeats to Senegal and Denmark.**

• Les Bleus returned to form in 2006, reaching the final in Germany where they lost on penalties to Italy. Sadly for his many admirers, the brilliant career of midfield maestro Zinedine Zidane ended on a low note as he was sent off for headbutting Italian defender Marco Materazzi.

• **France's campaign in 2010 was a chaotic affair, with the players briefly going on strike after forward Nicolas Anelka was ordered home by eccentric coach Raymond Domenech. Unsurprisingly, Les Bleus performed poorly on the pitch, picking up just a single point from their three group games against Uruguay, Mexico and hosts South Africa.**

PREVIOUS TOURNAMENTS

1930 Round 1	1966 Round 1	1994 Did not qualify
1934 Round 1	1970 Did not qualify	1998 Winners
1938 Round 2	1974 Did not qualify	2002 Round 1
1950 Did not qualify	1978 Round 1	2006 Runners-up
1954 Round 1	1982 Fourth place	2010 Round 1
1958 Third place	1986 Third place	
1962 Did not qualify	1990 Did not qualify	

HONDURAS

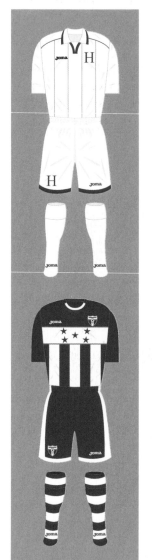

For the first time in their history Honduras will play at consecutive World Cups, having also appeared in South Africa in 2010. The Central Americans didn't exactly cover themselves in glory four years ago, failing to score a single goal and collecting just a solitary point as they finished last in their group, so they will be hoping for a better showing this summer.

Certainly, Honduras showed sufficient resilience and determination in qualification to suggest that they could be awkward group-phase opponents.

After starting their final pool campaign with three defeats in their opening six games their hopes of making it to Brazil looked slim indeed, but a sensational 2-1 victory away to Mexico proved to be a turning point and they eventually claimed the third automatic CONCACAF qualifying slot behind the USA and Costa Rica.

For Honduras coach Luis Fernando Suarez this will be his second World Cup, as he also guided Ecuador to the last 16 in Germany in 2006. He may struggle to match that achievement this time round, but he has a core of experienced players to call on who will not let him down. These include goalkeeper and captain Noel Valladores, Hull defender Maynor Figueroa and tough-tackling Stoke midfielder Wilson Palacios – a trio of grisled stalwarts whose combined number of caps exceeds 300.

Much of Honduras' attacking threat comes down the left, in the form of full-back Emilio Izaguirre. The Celtic man loves to get forward and will look to deliver his trademark pinpoint crosses for a pair of lively strikers: old hand Carlo Costly, once briefly of Birmingham City, and New England's Jerry Bengtson, his country's top scorer in qualification with nine goals.

Realistically, the pressure will be on that duo to hit the target as there is every chance that Honduras will find clean sheets hard to come by.

> **"I didn't want to face Ecuador."**
> Honduras coach Luis Fernando Suarez was disappointed to be drawn with his former team

HONDURAS AT THE WORLD CUP

• In 1969 Honduras were involved in the most violent episode in World Cup history when a series of three qualifying matches against neighbours El Salvador inflamed existing tensions between the two countries to such a pitch that a four-day war broke out. Around 3,000 people were killed in the so-called 'Soccer War' before international pressure brought about a ceasefire.

• **Honduras qualified for the finals for the first time in 1982. The Central American outfit did their nation proud, drawing 1-1 with both hosts Spain and Northern Ireland in their first two games before conceding a late penalty against Yugoslavia which ended their hopes of progressing into the second stage**.

• Honduras made World Cup history in South Africa in 2010 when they selected three brothers – Jerry, Johnny and Wilson Palacios – in their squad. It was a tournament to forget for the trio, though, as their country failed to score a single goal in their three games against Chile (1-0), Spain (2-0) and Switzerland (0-0).

PREVIOUS TOURNAMENTS

1930 Did not enter	1966 Did not qualify	1994 Did not qualify
1934 Did not enter	1970 Did not qualify	1998 Did not qualify
1938 Did not enter	1974 Did not qualify	2002 Did not qualify
1950 Did not enter	1978 Withdrew	2006 Did not qualify
1954 Did not enter	1982 Round 1	2010 Round 1
1958 Did not enter	1986 Did not qualify	
1962 Did not qualify	1990 Did not qualify	

KEY PLAYER

MAYNOR FIGUEROA

If, as seems likely, the Honduras defence comes under sustained pressure this summer then the central Americans will be looking to Hull City's Maynor Figueroa to organise their resistance to opposition attacks.

An experienced campaigner with over 100 caps who can operate either at left-back or as a centre-back, Figueroa first played for Honduras in 2003 and already has one World Cup under his belt, having appeared at the 2010 finals in South Africa.

At club level, Figueroa was a mainstay of the Wigan side which defied the odds to stay in the Premier League until they finally fell through the trapdoor in 2013. However, he remained in the top flight when he joined newly promoted Hull that summer.

A solid and uncompromising defender, Figueroa is also a threat from set pieces, as he famously demonstrated in the 2009/10 season when he scored with a fiercely-struck free-kick from just inside his own half against Stoke – a superb effort which was named the BBC's 'Goal of the Season'.

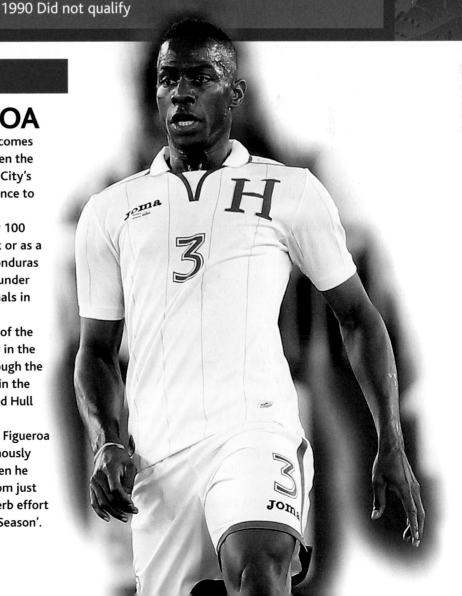

ARGENTINA

Any country that includes four-time World Player of the Year Lionel Messi in its ranks has to be considered serious contenders for the World Cup, but Argentina are far from being a one-man team. The South Americans are particularly strong in attacking positions, and promise to be one of the most exciting sides to watch in Brazil as they try to win the trophy for a third time after their previous successes in 1978 and 1986.

Messi and co. provided an indication of their awesome collective talent in the qualifying campaign, when they topped the South American group and scored a section-best 35 goals in total. It's no surprise, really, that Argentina demonstrated such impressive firepower as their strengths most definitely lie in the final third. Even coach Alejandro Sabella admits, "There's no doubt that we are better equipped in attack than in defence."

As well as Messi, Sabella can call on Manchester City goal machine Sergio Aguero, Napoli's prolific striker Gonzalo Higuain, Real Madrid's flying winger Angel di Maria and Valencia's creative midfielder Ever Banega. It's a truly frightening array of attacking talent.

There are, however, concerns about a defence which looked surprisingly vulnerable in some qualifying games. Goalkeeper Sergio Romero of Monaco struggles to deal with crosses, while the two central defenders, Napoli's Federico Fernandez and Benfica's Ezequiel Garay, are both relatively inexperienced. At least Argentina have an excellent right-back in the form of Manchester City's Pablo Zabaleta.

Given their defensive frailities it is, perhaps, fortunate that the Albicelestes (White and Sky Blues) have been drawn in a relatively easy group – which some of their more superstitious fans put down to "divine intervention" by Argentina's new man in the Vatican, Pope Francis. Even the Bishop of Rome, though, may be powerless to prevent Sabella's men from falling just short of a third title.

> **"We did not go into a group of death, there are other groups which are more complicated."**
> Argentina coach Alejandro Sabella

THE GAFFER:
ALEJANDRO SABELLA

When he was appointed Argentina manager in 2011 Alejandro Sabella identified one key task he needed to achieve: to get star player Lionel Messi performing as brilliantly for his country as he does so often for his club side, Barcelona.

"We must let him be happy," he said. "We must let him play completely freely on the pitch." The signs so far are good, with Messi appearing rejuvenated in the qualification campaign for Brazil, despite taking on the additional burden of team captain.

With Argentina comfortably topping the South American qualifying section for this summer's finals, Sabella has got off to a good start in international management. The 59-year-old, though, is no novice at the top level, having previously served as Daniel Passarella's assistant when the 1978 World Cup-winning captain was in charge of Argentina and Uruguay in the 1990s. Sabella later became head coach at Estudiantes, leading them to the Copa Libertadores in 2009.

A creative midfielder who was nicknamed 'El Mago' ('The Magician') in his playing days, Sabella spent most of his career with Argentinian clubs River Plate and Estudiantes. He also had a fondly remembered three-year spell in England with Sheffield United and Leeds between 1978 and 1981.

KEY PLAYER

LIONEL MESSI

World Player of the Year on a record four occasions, Lionel Messi is rated by many as the greatest footballer ever.

Famed for his superb control, mesmeric dribbling skills and prolific goalscoring ability, the Barcelona wizard has won a host of silverware in his club career, including Champions League medals and La Liga titles. Along the way, Messi has smashed numerous records, most notably rising to the top of Barcelona's all-time goalscoring list when he banged in goal number 233 against Getafe in March 2012.

However, at international level Messi has not quite hit the same heights. He did win gold with Argentina at the 2008 Olympics in Beijing, but he failed to make a major impression at either the 2006 or 2010 World Cups. Given more of a free role by coach Alejandro Sabella in the qualifiers for Brazil, though, Messi was in stunning form, scoring 10 goals and weaving past defenders as if they didn't exist.

Now captain of his country, the 2014 finals are Messi's moment to shine on the world stage.

ONE TO WATCH: SERGIO AGUERO

At just five feet and eight inches, Sergio Aguero may be one of the smallest strikers at this summer's finals but there's every chance he will be among the deadliest.

For one thing, the Manchester City man is much tougher than he appears at first sight, earning praise from his national team captain Lionel Messi for his "immense power, strength and incredible work ethic". Add to those qualities Aguero's superb close ball control and poacher's instincts inside the box and you have a marksman of the highest order.

Known as 'El Kun' because of his resemblance to the Japanese cartoon character, Kum Kum, Aguero started out with Argentinian side Independiente before joining Atletico Madrid in 2006. He won the inaugural Europa League with the Spanish giants in 2010, but moved on to Manchester City the following year. After helping City win the FA Cup in 2011, he then scored the decisive goal the next year as City won the Premier League on the last day of the season.

At international level, Aguero was part of the Argentina side that won gold at the Olympic Games in Beijing in 2008.

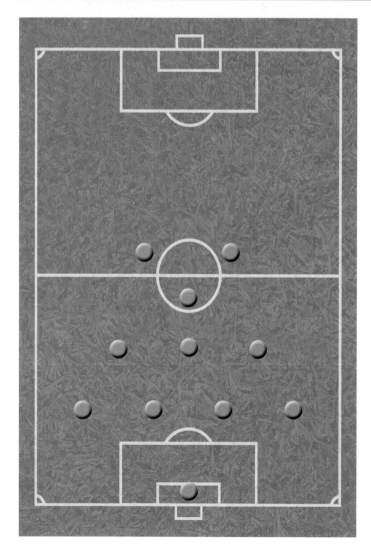

TACTICS BOARD

MAKING MESSI MAYHEM

Opposition coaches at the World Cup finals this summer will not be surprised to learn that Argentina's main plan is to get the ball as often as possible to Lionel Messi, and then let the little magician take it from there.

Alejandro Sabella's skill has been to structure his team in such a way that when Messi gains possession he has players ahead of him who can accept a telling pass or, maybe, play a devastating one-two with the Barcelona genius. To this end, Sabella has decided that Argentina are most dangerous when they field two strikers, Gonzalo Higuain and Sergio Aguero, in front of Messi in a 4-3-1-2 formation.

Behind the trio of attackers, Fernando Gago and Javier Mascherano do the dirty work in midfield, while Real Madrid's Angel di Maria provides more creativity on the left. Additional width, meanwhile, comes from the full-backs with Manchester City's Pablo Zabaleta being the biggest threat on the right.

ARGENTINA AT THE WORLD CUP

• Argentina played in the first ever World Cup final, losing 4-2 to neighbours Uruguay in Montevideo. The result didn't go down well in Buenos Aires, where an angry crowd threw stones at the Uruguayan Consulate until they were dispersed by gun-wielding police.

• **After a 24-year absence Argentina returned to the finals in 1958, but a tactically inept side were thrashed 6-1 by Czechoslovakia and finished bottom of their group. As if that wasn't bad enough, the players were pelted with coins and vegetables by angry fans on their return from Sweden.**

• At the 1966 tournament in England, Argentina were involved in one of the most notorious matches in World Cup history. Playing the hosts at Wembley in the quarter-finals, Argentina captain Antonio Rattin was sent off in the first half, but initially refused to leave the pitch. After an extremely physical match, which Argentina lost 1-0, England manager Alf Ramsey called the South Americans "animals".

• **Argentina hosted the tournament for the first time in 1978 and thrilled their fanatical fans by reaching the final, where they beat the Netherlands 3-1. Long-haired striker Mario Kempes was the hero of the hour, scoring**

It took more than three Belgian defenders to stop Diego Maradona in 1986

two of his side's goals as they won in extra-time.

• Argentina won the tournament for a second time in 1986, thanks mainly to their inspirational captain Diego Maradona. In the quarter-final against England Maradona scored two goals, one a brilliant solo effort and the other punched in with his fist – although he later cheekily claimed that it was scored with the 'Hand of God'. He banged in another brace in the semi-final against Belgium and then set up Jorge Burruchaga for the winner against West Germany in the final.

• **Four years later Argentina reached the final again in Italy, but were beaten 1-0 by West** Germany. **In the 65th minute Argentina's Pedro Monzon became the first player to be sent off in the World Cup final and was followed by team-mate Gustavo Dezotti, who received a red card in the dying minutes.**

• Germany have become Argentina's least favourite opponents at recent World Cups. In 2006 Jurgen Klinsmann's side beat the South Americans on penalties in the quarter-finals. Four years later the teams met again in South Africa at the same stage. Argentina, coached by the legendary Maradona, had started the tournament in fine style but they were outclassed by Germany on the day, going down to a 4-0 defeat.

PREVIOUS TOURNAMENTS

1930 Runners-up	1966 Quarter-finals	1994 Round 2
1934 Round 1	1970 Did not qualify	1998 Quarter-finals
1938 Withdrew	1974 Round 2	2002 Round 1
1950 Did not enter	1978 Winners	2006 Quarter-finals
1954 Did not enter	1982 Round 2	2010 Quarter-finals
1958 Round 1	1986 Winners	
1962 Round 1	1990 Runners-up	

BOSNIA-HERCEGOVINA

The only one of the 32 competing nations who will be playing at their first World Cup finals, Bosnia-Hercegovina's qualification for this summer's football festival was greeted with scenes of ecstatic celebration in the capital Sarajevo. For those Bosnians old enough to remember the terrible war which engulfed the Balkan country 18 years ago, the team's achievement represented much more than a mere sporting triumph.

Bosnia's success was founded on goals – and plenty of them. The team topped their qualifying group ahead of Greece on goal difference, after netting an impressive 30 times in their 10 games – a tally which was only bettered by England, Germany and the Netherlands in the European qualifying section. The deadly strike pairing of Manchester City's Edin Dzeko and Stuttgart's Vedad Ibisevic contributed 18 of those goals between them, the latter hitting the vital winner in Lithuania which booked Bosnia's passage to the World Cup. The duo will take some stopping this summer.

Behind them, veteran playmaker Zvjezdan Misimovic is often at the heart of Bosnia's most fluent moves. A league title winner with Wolfsburg in 2009, he now plies his trade in China and will view the finals as a last opportunity to show his skills on the international stage, after just missing out on the 2010 World Cup and Euro 2012 when Bosnia were beaten in the play-offs.

Misimovic is likely to be supported in head coach Safet Susic's attractive 4-1-3-2 formation by two Italian-based players, Roma's Miralem Pjanic and Lazio's Senad Lulic and, in the midfield holding role, a former Netherlands Under-21 international in Haris Medunjanin.

Bosnia's defence, meanwhile, is built around Stoke City's reliable goalkeeper Asmir Begovic and experienced team captain Emir Spahic of Bayer Leverkusen. However, if Dzeko and Ibisevic are on form in Brazil, it will surely be their attack that catches the eye of the neutral.

> **"We'll be doing everything we can to make Bosnia-Hercegovina proud."**
> Prolific Bosnia striker Vedad Ibisevic

BOSNIA-HERCEGOVINA AT THE WORLD CUP

• A country born out of the violent break-up of the old Yugoslavia in the early 1990s, Bosnia-Hercegovina first attempted to qualify for the 1998 World Cup in France. Despite having to play against Croatia in Bologna because of political tensions between the two countries they did well, finishing third.

• **Bosnia came even closer in the qualification process for the** last World Cup in South Africa, **finishing second behind eventual winners Spain to set up a two-legged play-off with Portugal. Unfortunately for the Bosnians, they lost both games 1-0 to see their World Cup qualification hopes dashed.**

• Bosnia striker Edin Dzeko's nine goals in the qualifying games for the 2010 World Cup made him the joint-second highest scorer in the UEFA section, one behind Greece's Theofanis Gekas.

• **In qualifying for the 2014 finals in Brazil, Bosnia recorded their biggest ever win – an 8-1 demolition of Liechtenstein. Strikers Dzeko and Vedad Ibisevic both scored hat-tricks against the hapless minnows, to leave the pair arguing over the match ball.**

PREVIOUS TOURNAMENTS

1930-90 Competed as part of Yugoslavia
1994 Could not enter

1998 Did not qualify
2002 Did not qualify
2006 Did not qualify

2010 Did not qualify

KEY PLAYER

EDIN DZEKO

Bosnia's highest ever scorer with over 30 goals for his country, Edin Dzeko was on target 10 times during his team's successful World Cup qualification campaign – making him the second highest goalscorer in the UEFA section behind the Netherlands' prolific striker, Robin van Persie.

Tall, powerful and a reliable finisher both on the ground and in the air, Dzeko made his name with Wolfsburg with whom he won the Bundesliga title in 2009, contributing 26 goals. The following season he topped the league's goalscoring charts with 22 goals.

Such form inevitably caught the attention of the Premier League's elite clubs and in January 2011 Dzeko moved to Manchester City for £27 million, making him the most expensive ever export from a German club.

'The Bosnian Diamond', as he is known in his native country, has continued to find the target regularly in England despite often being used as a substitute. Dzeko helped City win the FA Cup against Stoke in 2011 and then the Premier League title the following year when he scored the vital late equaliser before Sergio Aguero's heroics in the final game against QPR.

IRAN

Playing at their fourth World Cup, Iran will be hoping to progress to the knockout stages for the first time in their history. Their chances, though, have to be rated as remote given the tricky group they have been drawn in. Nonetheless, the Asian side are sure to put up dogged resistance and will be well-organised by their highly respected coach, former Real Madrid boss Carlos Queiroz.

In charge of the Iranians since 2011, Queiroz is a vastly experienced figure, having previously managed Portugal, the United Arab Emirates and South Africa, as well as enjoying two successful spells as Sir Alex's Ferguson's assistant at Manchester United. This will be his second World Cup as he took Portugal to the 2010 tournament in South Africa, but was sacked a few months after their second-round exit to eventual winners Spain.

Queiroz will do well to take Iran as far against Argentina, Bosnia-Hercegovina and Nigeria. 'Team Melli', as fans call the national side, are completely lacking in star names and the squad is largely composed of players from Iran's two biggest clubs, Esteghlal and Persepolis. They are, though, a difficult side to break down, as they showed by conceding just two goals in their eight final pool qualifying games against South Korea, Uzbekistan, Qatar and Lebanon.

Among their most important players are goalkeeper Rahman Ahmadi, defensive stalwart Jalal Hosseini, Fulham attacking midfielder Askan Dejagah, skipper Javad Nekounam, and striker Reza Ghoochannejhad, on loan at Charlton. A recent addition to the squad, Ghoochannejhad had previously played for the Netherlands' youth team after emigrating to Europe with his parents as a child. After opting to play for his homeland, though, he became an instant hero to millions of his fellow Iranians when he scored the winner in South Korea that booked his country's passage to Brazil.

> "It's a great opportunity for us to progress and be a better team."
>
> Iran coach
> Carlos Queiroz

IRAN AT THE WORLD CUP

• Iran first competed at the World Cup in 1978 in Argentina. After losing 3-0 to the Netherlands in their opening fixture, the Iranians then pulled off a major surprise when they managed to hold Scotland to a 1-1 draw. After that, it didn't really matter that Iran were thrashed 4-1 by Peru in their final group match.

• Two decades later, Iran beat Australia – managed by former England boss Terry Venables – in a play-off on the away goals rule to qualify for the 1998 tournament in France. Iran began their campaign with a narrow defeat to Yugoslavia, but much better was to come.

• In their next fixture the Iranians recorded a 2-1 victory over the USA – a country dubbed 'The Great Satan' by Iran's hardline Islamic government – to spark ecstatic celebrations back in Tehran. A 2-0 defeat at the hands of Germany, though, ended their hopes of getting out of the group.

• Iran striker Ali Daei scored a record 35 goals in World Cup qualifiers between 1994 and 2006.

PREVIOUS TOURNAMENTS

1930 Did not enter	1966 Did not enter	1994 Did not qualify
1934 Did not enter	1970 Did not enter	1998 Round 1
1938 Did not enter	1974 Did not qualify	2002 Did not qualify
1950 Did not enter	1978 Round 1	2006 Round 1
1954 Did not enter	1982 Withdrew	2010 Did not qualify
1958 Did not enter	1986 Disqualified	
1962 Did not enter	1990 Did not qualify	

KEY PLAYER

JAVAD NEKOUNAM

Now aged 33, Iran captain Javad Nekounam may be in the latter stages of his career but his experience will be crucial to his side this summer.

An intelligent all-round midfielder who passes the ball accurately, tackles ferociously and carries a genuine goal threat, Nekounam moved from Al-Sharjah in the United Arab Emirates to Osasuna after impressing at the 2006 World Cup in Germany. He spent six years in Spain, gaining rave reviews for his committed performances before joining Iran's leading club, Esteghlal, and is now on loan at Kuwait Sporting Club.

After making his international debut way back in 2000, Nekounam helped Iran win the Asian Games two years later. He has gone on to win more than 130 caps for his country, making him the second highest appearance maker in Iranian football history, and was an influential figure in his team's qualification for Brazil this summer.

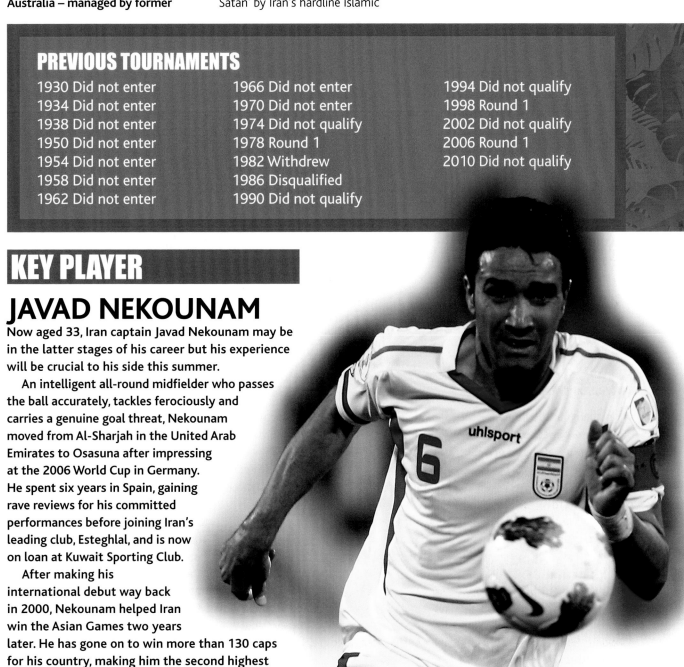

NIGERIA

As champions of their continent, following a 1-0 victory over Burkina Faso in the final of the 2013 African Nations Cup, Nigeria will travel to Brazil full of confidence. The Super Eagles will fancy their chances of going as far, if not further, than any other African side as they aim to improve on their second-round efforts of 1994 and 1998. However, they might have preferred not to have been drawn with Argentina for the fourth time since their World Cup debut in 1994.

Under coach Stephen Keshi, one of just two people to have won the African Nations Cup both as a player and manager, Nigeria have developed into a decent all-round side that likes to keep possession of the ball and hit opponents with sudden attacks from deep-lying positions. This strategy was shown to good effect in the play-offs, as the Super Eagles comfortably disposed of Ethiopia over two legs.

> **"We will respect all the teams and take it game after game."**
> Nigeria assistant coach Daniel Amokachi

The key players for Nigeria from a defensive point of view are vastly experienced Lille goalkeeper Victor Enyeama and Celtic centre-back Efe Ambrose.

There may also be a starting place for young Chelsea defender Kenneth Omeruo who, despite a lack of Premier League action, has impressed in his first appearances for the Africans.

The Chelsea connections continue in midfield where John Mikel Obi and Victor Moses will benefit from having played together at club level. Perhaps, though, Nigeria's most exciting talent in this area of the pitch is CSKA Moscow's pocket-sized playmaker Ahmed Musa. He will look to link with second striker Victor Obinna, once of West Ham but now with Lokomotiv Moscow, and main target man Emmanuel Emenike of Fenerbahce. Meanwhile, Newcastle veteran Shola Ameobi, a former England Under-21 international, is most likely to feature from the bench.

Argentina aside, Nigeria's group is not especially daunting and they have every opportunity of progressing to the knockout stages.

NIGERIA AT THE WORLD CUP

• Nigeria first competed at the World Cup finals in the USA in 1994 and gave their fans back home plenty to cheer. After victories against Bulgaria and Greece ensured their passage into the knockout phase, the Super Eagles came close to eliminating eventual finalists Italy in the last 16 before two goals by pony-tailed striker Roberto Baggio condemned them to a 2-1 defeat after extra-time.

• **Nigeria also made it out of the group stage at the 1998 finals in France, this time thanks to victories over Spain and Bulgaria. However, a poor display in the last 16 against Denmark saw the Africans slump to an emphatic 4-1 defeat.**

• At the 2002 finals in Japan and South Korea the Super Eagles fared less well, only managing a solitary point from a dull 0-0 draw with England, having already been eliminated following defeats by Argentina and Sweden.

• It was a similar story in South Africa eight years later, the Super Eagles flying home early with a solitary point to show from a 2-2 draw with South Korea after defeats by both Japan (1-0) and Denmark (2-1).

PREVIOUS TOURNAMENTS

1930 Did not enter	1966 Withdrew	1994 Round 2
1934 Did not enter	1970 Did not qualify	1998 Round 2
1938 Did not enter	1974 Did not qualify	2002 Round 1
1950 Did not enter	1978 Did not qualify	2006 Did not qualify
1954 Did not enter	1982 Did not qualify	2010 Round 1
1958 Did not enter	1986 Did not qualify	
1962 Did not qualify	1990 Did not qualify	

KEY PLAYER

JOHN MIKEL OBI

An often underrated player, John Mikel Obi's calm efficiency in possession and ability to pass the ball accurately over short and medium distances provides the platform for Nigeria's more creative talents to flourish.

Mikel's worth to his club side, Chelsea, has certainly been proven over the years, as he has helped the Blues win a host of silverware – including the Champions League in 2012 – since joining the Londoners from Norwegian club Lyn in 2006. His time at Stamford Bridge, though, has been marked by some controversial incidents, most notably when he was fined £60,000 after threatening referee Mark Clattenburg following a bad-tempered defeat by Manchester United in October 2012.

With Nigeria, Mikel enjoyed his best moment in 2013, when he was voted man of the match while helping his country beat Burkina Faso in the final of the African Nations Cup. He was runner-up in the 2013 African Player of the Year award.

GERMANY

Three-time winners of the World Cup, Germany have an unmatched record of consistent achievement at the finals, only once failing to reach the last eight in their 17 tournament appearances. It is, though, a while since the Germans actually got their hands on some silverware – their last triumph coming at Euro '96. For a country so used to success the 18 years since then will feel like a lifetime, so the pressure is on Joachim Low's team in Brazil.

However, there are definite signs that the Germans can improve even on their last World Cup showing, when they came third in South Africa. For a start, their qualification campaign was deeply impressive, with nine wins out of 10 – the only blot on their copybook being a draw with Sweden when, uncharacteristically, they let slip a 4-0 lead. The Germans were also the highest scorers in the European qualifying section with 36 goals, Arsenal's attacking midfielder Mesut Ozil leading the way with seven.

Stats aside, Germany simply have a wonderful squad, stuffed full of talented, dynamic and tactically aware players from 2013 Champions League finalists Bayern Munich and Borussia Dortmund. Bayern goalkeeper Manuel Neuer is one of the best in the world in his position, while the defence also boasts skipper Philipp Lahm and experienced Arsenal centre-back Per Mertesacker.

In midfield, Low has numerous top-notch options, including Ozil and Bayern veteran Bastian Schweinsteiger. Meanwhile, Bayern's Thomas Muller and Dortmund's Marco Reus are a pair of brilliant wide players.

Perhaps the one problematic position for Low is at centre-forward. Miroslav Klose, now with Lazio, remains the first choice but he will be 36 at the finals. Too old? Maybe. But you just know that if Klose wilts in the heat of Brazil, the Germans will find another solution – because that's what they always do.

> **"Our opponents are old friends, we played Ghana in 2010 and Portugal at Euro 2012."**
> Germany coach
> Joachim Low

THE GAFFER: JOACHIM LOW

The second-longest serving national team manager at this summer's finals, Joachim Low was appointed Germany boss after the 2006 World Cup having previously served as Jurgen Klinsmann's assistant.

In his eight years in the top job, Low has made steady progress, bringing in talented younger players to blend in with the older heads while continuing to develop his offensive-minded philosophy. Thus far, ultimate success has proved elusive, although Low has been far from a flop. In 2008 he guided Germany to the final of the European Championships, where they lost 1-0 to Spain. Further near misses came at the 2010 World Cup and the 2012 European Championships, Germany reaching the semi-finals of both competitions. Throughout his tenure, the tactically astute Low has stressed to his players the importance of moving the ball quickly and accurately, making the Germans arguably the most deadly counter-attacking side in world football.

A jobbing midfielder in his playing days with Freiburg, Eintracht Frankfurt and Karlsruhe, Low started out in management with Stuttgart, taking them to the final of the 1998 European Cup Winners' Cup – which they lost 1-0 to Chelsea. He later managed in Turkey and Austria, leading Tirol Innsbruck to the league title in 2002.

KEY PLAYER

PHILIPP LAHM

Pint-sized Germany captain Phillip Lahm is his country's 'Mr Versatile', equally at home playing at full-back or in a defensive midfield role and rarely dropping below the consistently excellent standards he sets himself.

One of just nine German players to pass the 100-cap mark, Lahm is a veteran of both the 2006 and 2010 World Cups, and was voted into the Team of the Tournament in South Africa four years ago. He was also a member of the Germany side that reached the final of the European Championships in 2008.

Lahm came through the Bayern Munich youth system to make his debut for the Bavarian giants in 2002. Since then the 'Magic Dwarf', as he is known to the Bayern fans, has gone on to win a hatful of Bundesliga titles and the Champions League.

Often underrated by the media, Lahm was singled out for high praise when former Barcelona coach Pep Guardiola joined Bayern in the summer of 2013. "He is perhaps the most intelligent player I have ever trained in my career," said the Spaniard. "He is at another level."

ONE TO WATCH: THOMAS MULLER

At 24 Thomas Muller has already achieved more in the game than most players manage in their entire careers.

A product of the Bayern Munich youth system, Muller came through the ranks to become a key member of the side that won the domestic Double and reached the Champions League final in 2010 – only to lose to Jose Mourinho's Inter Milan. Muller endured more Champions League heartache two years later when, despite scoring with a header against Chelsea in the final in Munich, he again finished on the losing side. However, he finally got his hands on Europe's top club prize in 2013 when Bayern beat fellow Germans Borussia Dortmund in the final at Wembley, after Muller had starred in the 7-0 aggregate thrashing of Barcelona in the semi-finals, scoring three of his side's goals.

A powerful runner who is strong in the air and possesses a fearsome shot, Muller performed superbly in the 2010 World Cup in South Africa, scoring five goals – including two in a 4-1 demolition of England in the last 16 – and making three assists to win the Golden Boot.

TACTICS BOARD

FORWARD MOVEMENT

Essentially a counter-attacking side in the past, Germany have evolved to become more of a short-passing team in recent years, with the accent put on moving the ball quickly and in a forward direction. Coach Joachim Low still employs a 4-2-3-1 system but, with one of the defensive midfielders often pushing into more advanced positions, the actual formation on the pitch can be closer to 4-1-4-1.

Playing just behind veteran striker Miroslav Klose, Arsenal's Mesut Ozil is a key player as his guile and creativity can create opportunities for the Lazio man or the wide attackers, Bayern Munich's Thomas Muller and Borussia Dortmund's Marco Reus.

Once a tireless midfield runner, Bastian Schweinsteiger is now the anchor in front of the defence, which is marshalled by the towering Per Mertesacker. Out on the flanks, meanwhile, both full-backs, skipper Philipp Lahm and Dortmund's Marcel Schmelzer, love to get forward to support the German attacks.

GERMANY AT THE WORLD CUP

• Germany first competed at the World Cup in 1934 and performed reasonably well, reaching the semi-finals before losing 3-1 to Czechoslovakia in Rome.

• **After being banned by FIFA from the 1950 tournament as a punishment for starting World War II, Germany returned to the world stage in 1954 (as West Germany) and won the trophy for the first time after coming from 2-0 down to beat Hungary 3-2 in the final in Berne. The result was a major surprise as the Hungarians had earlier trounced the Germans 8-3 in a group game.**

'Der Kaiser' Franz Beckenbauer lifts the 1974 World Cup

• West Germany reached the final for a second time in 1966, but went down 4-2 to hosts England at Wembley after extra-time. Nearly 50 years on, the Germans still complain that England's controversial third goal didn't actually cross the line.

• **Eight years later the Germans claimed the trophy for a second time when, as hosts, they beat the Netherlands 2-1 in Munich. Prolific striker Gerd 'der Bomber' Muller was the home side's hero, netting the winner after both teams had scored from the penalty spot.**

• In 1982 West Germany reached the final for a fourth time, after beating France in the semi-finals in the first ever World Cup shoot-out.

However, a 3-1 defeat at the hands of Italy meant they went home without the trophy.

• **Four years later West Germany were back in the final but lost again, this time going down 3-2 to an Argentina side inspired by their brilliant captain, Diego Maradona.**

• The same two sides met again in the 1990 final in Rome, the Germans winning a bad-tempered match thanks to a late penalty by defender Andreas Brehme. The team's coach, 1974 World Cup-winning captain Franz Beckenbauer, became only the second person to win the trophy as both a player and manager.

• **After shock quarter-final defeats by Bulgaria in 1994 and Croatia four years later, Germany reached their seventh final in 2002. The Germans had been indebted to their goalkeeper, Oliver Kahn, in previous matches but his blunder gifted Brazil their first goal in an eventual 2-0 victory in Yokohama.**

• Hosting the tournament in 2006 and coached by 1990 World Cup winner Jurgen Klinsmann, Germany reached the semi-finals but went down 2-0 to eventual champions Italy. It was a similar story in South Africa in 2010, as the Germans made it to the last four for a record 12th time only to lose to Spain.

PREVIOUS TOURNAMENTS

1930 Did not enter	1966 Runners-up	1994 Quarter-finals
1934 Third place	1970 Third place	1998 Quarter-finals
1938 Round 1	1974 Winners	2002 Runners-up
1950 Banned	1978 Round 2	2006 Third place
1954 Winners	1982 Runners-up	2010 Third place
1958 Fourth place	1986 Runners-up	
1962 Quarter-finals	1990 Winners	

PORTUGAL

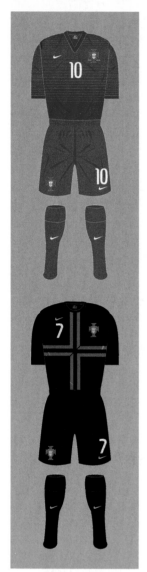

With the brilliant Cristiano Ronaldo in their line-up, Portugal will be a threat to any side in Brazil. The southern Europeans, though, are far from being a one-man team as they showed by reaching the semi-finals of Euro 2012 where they lost on penalties to eventual champions Spain. With a squad boasting a number of players from various top Spanish outfits they have the all-round quality to go far in the tournament.

It's certainly true, however, that the Portuguese were indebted to Ronaldo in the play-offs, when he scored all of their goals in a dramatic 4-2 aggregate win over Sweden, in what seemed at times like a personal battle with Zlatan Ibrahimovic. Coach Paulo Bento will be keen to see other players stepping up to the plate alongside 'CR7' this summer, especially as Portugal have been drawn in an extremely tricky group.

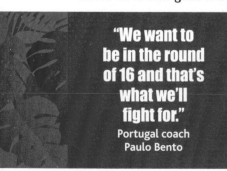

"We want to be in the round of 16 and that's what we'll fight for."
Portugal coach Paulo Bento

He should have few worries, though, as Portugal have decent ability in all areas of the pitch. The defence is solid, with Bruno Alves and Pepe forming a combative central partnership while Real Madrid's Fabio Coentrao and Valencia's Joao Pereira both like to get forward from full-back. In midfield, Monaco's Joao Moutinho is the brains of the team and a creative passer of the ball, while former Chelsea man Raul Meireles and Dynamo Kiev's Miguel Veloso are two tireless dogsbodies.

Lone striker Helder Postiga is not a world-class finisher, but chipped in with six valuable goals in qualifying. He will hope for good service from wingers Ronaldo and Nani, although if the latter doesn't improve on his patchy club form even more of the burden will fall on the Real Madrid star.

As ever with Portugal, much will depend on Ronaldo. He will be a marked man in Brazil, but such is his talent that he will only need to escape the defensive shackles occasionally to lead his team out of a tough group at the very least.

THE GAFFER: PAULO BENTO

Appointed Portugal coach in September 2010, Paulo Bento's career in international management got off to a superb start when his side hammered world champions Spain 4-0 in a friendly in Lisbon in only his third match in charge.

Since then he has gone from strength to strength, guiding Portugal to the semi-finals of Euro 2012 – where they were slightly unlucky to lose to Spain on penalties – and to the World Cup finals in Brazil after a thrilling play-off victory against Sweden.

A gritty defensive midfielder in his playing days, Bento turned out for Lisbon giants Benfica and Sporting with a four-year stint at Oviedo in Spain in between. He was also part of the so-called 'Golden Generation' Portugal team which was highly fancied at the 2002 World Cup, but returned home after the group phase.

Three years later Bento was appointed first-team coach of Sporting Lisbon. He enjoyed a good deal of success with the club, leading them to two Portuguese Cup triumphs and securing regular Champions League football. However, a record 12-1 aggregate defeat by Bayern Munich in the last 16 in March 2009 allied to fan criticisms of Bento's defensive tactics led to his resignation later that year.

KEY PLAYER

CRISTIANO RONALDO

Arguably the most exciting attacking player in world football, Cristiano Ronaldo is central to Portugal's hopes at this summer's World Cup.

The 2013 World Player of the Year dragged his country to Brazil almost single-handedly, scoring the winner with a diving header in the first leg of the play-off against Sweden and then smashing a sensational hat-trick in the return.

Performances like that have been a feature of the winger's career since he started out with Sporting Lisbon more than a decade ago. After catching the eye of Sir Alex Ferguson, Ronaldo moved to Manchester United in 2003 where he won a host of silverware, including the Champions League in 2008, before joining Real Madrid in a world record £80 million deal the next year. He enjoyed his best season with the Spanish giants in 2011/12, his club record 46 league goals helping Real win La Liga.

Captain of Portugal since 2007, Ronaldo has already passed the 100-cap mark and is odds on to be both his country's highest appearance maker and top scorer when he finally hangs up his boots.

ONE TO WATCH: PEPE

A no-nonsense hardman who can perform equally well in central defence or in a holding midfield role, Pepe was born in Brazil but became a Portuguese national in 2007.

He made his international debut in November that year, and has since gone on to represent Portugal at two European Championships and the 2010 World Cup. Now aged 31 and with nearly 60 caps to his name, he will be one of the most experienced Portuguese players at the finals in Brazil.

Real name Kepler Laveran Lima Ferreira, Pepe has enjoyed huge success at club level, winning back-to-back titles with Porto before joining Real Madrid for around £20 million in 2007. In his first season with the Spanish giants he won the league title, a feat he repeated in 2012.

For all his achievements, though, Pepe is probably best known for his appalling disciplinary record. Most famously, he was given a 10-match ban in 2009 for stamping on a Getafe player he had already brutally chopped down in the penalty area and then punching another player in the face as he walked off the pitch.

TACTICS BOARD
ROAMING RONNIE

A dangerous counter-attacking side, Portugal will line up in Brazil in a 4-3-3 formation designed to get the best out of their star player, Cristiano Ronaldo.

Although he will start on the left, Ronaldo has licence to roam pretty much wherever he pleases in the final third. With the Portuguese captain likely to attract the attention of two or even three opponents, the plan is to change the point of the attack swiftly to allow the likes of right-winger Nani and lone striker Helder Postiga to exploit any defensive gaps.

In Portugal's midfield, Joao Moutinho is the playmaker who keeps the side ticking over. He is supported by two box-to-box midfielders, the heavily-tattooed Raul Meireles and Dynamo Kiev's Miguel Veloso, who both enjoy shooting from the edge of the area.

In front of reliable goalkeeper Rui Patricio, meanwhile, old stagers Bruno Alves and Pepe organise a defence which delights in taking no prisoners.

PORTUGAL AT THE WORLD CUP

• Portugal didn't appear at the World Cup until 1966, but they made up for lost time by reaching the semi-finals. Up against hosts England at Wembley, the Portuguese gave a good account of themselves before losing 2-1. In the previous round against surprise packages North Korea, Portugal made one of the greatest comebacks at the finals, fighting back from 3-0 down at Goodison Park to win 5-3.

• **The brilliant Eusebio, arguably Portugal's greatest ever player, banged in four goals in that game, and with nine goals in total was the tournament's leading scorer.**

• Portugal didn't reach the finals again until 1986, and they qualified for the finals in Mexico in superb style with a 1-0 victory away to West Germany in Stuttgart – the first time that the Germans had been beaten at home in a competitive fixture.

• **Portugal began the tournament proper with an excellent 1-0 win over England, thanks to a late goal by Carlos Manuel. However, a dispute over prize money undermined the team's collective spirit and after consecutive defeats to Poland and Morocco they were knocked out.**

• The Portuguese had another long wait before returning to the finals, but finally did so in 2002 with

Cristiano Ronaldo takes the plaudits as England depart the 2006 World Cup

a fine team dubbed the 'Golden Generation'. Sadly for their fans, Luis Figo and co. failed to deliver when it really mattered, losing to both the USA and co-hosts South Korea between a 4-0 thrashing of Poland that demonstrated what the side was capable of on a good day.

• **At the 2006 finals in Germany, Portugal were involved in the dirtiest match in World Cup history against the Netherlands in the last 16. Overworked Russian referee Valentin Ivanov sent off four players and booked 16 in a match that the Portuguese won 1-0. They then beat England on** penalties thanks to the heroics of goalkeeper Ricardo, who saved spot-kicks from Frank Lampard, Steven Gerrard and Jamie Carragher. In the semi-finals, though, Portugal lost by a single goal to France.

• In South Africa in 2010 Portugal recorded their biggest ever win at the finals – a 7-0 tonking of minnows North Korea. That victory helped the Portuguese advance to the last 16, where they came up against neighbours Spain. In a closely-fought encounter, a solitary goal by David Villa was enough to see the Spanish through.

PREVIOUS TOURNAMENTS

1930 Did not enter	1966 Third place	1994 Did not qualify
1934 Did not qualify	1970 Did not qualify	1998 Did not qualify
1938 Did not qualify	1974 Did not qualify	2002 Round 1
1950 Did not qualify	1978 Did not qualify	2006 Fourth place
1954 Did not qualify	1982 Did not qualify	2010 Round 2
1958 Did not qualify	1986 Round 1	
1962 Did not qualify	1990 Did not qualify	

GHANA

Ghana captivated football fans across the globe at the last World Cup, swaggering their way into the quarter-finals and narrowly missing out on becoming the first African side to reach the last four when they lost to Uruguay in a penalty shoot-out. The Black Stars will be keen to build on that experience in Brazil, but they may struggle to progress from a frighteningly difficult group.

Still, Ghana will travel to South America buoyed by an excellent qualifying campaign which saw them top their original group ahead of 2012 African Nations Cup champions Zambia and then crush Egypt 7-3 in the play-offs. Their success meant that coach Kwesi Appiah became the first ever black African to lead Ghana to the World Cup finals.

> **"I think we've landed in the group of death."**
> Ghana coach Kwesi Appiah

Appiah is a huge admirer of Arsenal's close passing style, and has enough quality performers in his squad to realise his ambition of turning the Black Stars into a passable imitation of the free-flowing Gunners. This is particularly the case in midfield, where Appiah can draw on the power of AC Milan's Michael Essien, the subtle touches of his club team-mate Sulley Muntari and the goal threat of Kevin-Prince Boateng. Intriguingly, the German-born Schalke player may face his brother, Bayern Munich defender Jerome Boateng, when Ghana meet Germany in their second fixture.

Ghana were the most prolific African side in qualifying, scoring 25 goals in total, and their attack certainly has the ability to trouble their opponents' defences this summer. Andre Ayew of Marseille and Christian Atsu of Vitesse could both feature in this department.

However, the main man will undoubtedly be captain Asamoah Gyan. He will be desperate to atone for his costly penalty miss against Uruguay in the quarter-finals four years ago, and will be key to his country's chances of escaping from their forbidding group.

GHANA AT THE WORLD CUP

• Ghana first competed at the World Cup in 2006 and surprised many by reaching the second round – the only African side to do so. The Black Stars beat both the Czech Republic and the USA to make it out of their group, but were then paired with holders Brazil in the last 16 and went down to a 3-0 defeat.

• **At the 2010 tournament in South Africa Ghana performed even better, finishing second in their group ahead of Australia on goal difference.**

• In the last 16 Ghana beat USA 2-1, with Asamoah Gyan grabbing the winner, to set up a quarter-final tie with Uruguay. With the scores level at 1-1 deep into extra-time Uruguay striker Luis Suarez palmed away a goalbound header, giving Gyan the opportunity from the penalty spot to send Ghana into the semi-finals – a feat never before achieved by an African country.

• **With a whole continent willing him to score, Gyan smashed his shot against the crossbar and Uruguay went on to win the subsequent penalty shoot-out to end Ghana's involvement in the tournament.**

PREVIOUS TOURNAMENTS

1930 Did not enter	1966 Withdrew	1994 Did not qualify
1934 Did not enter	1970 Did not qualify	1998 Did not qualify
1938 Did not enter	1974 Did not qualify	2002 Did not qualify
1950 Did not enter	1978 Did not qualify	2006 Round 2
1954 Did not enter	1982 Withdrew	2010 Quarter-finals
1958 Did not enter	1986 Did not qualify	
1962 Did not enter	1990 Did not qualify	

KEY PLAYER

ASAMOAH GYAN

A livewire striker who enjoys playing on the shoulder of the last defender, Asamoah Gyan is the man most likely to fire Ghana beyond the group stages in Brazil. And, having got on the scoresheet at two previous World Cups, the forward will certainly not be lacking in confidence when the tournament kicks off.

Nonetheless, Gyan will have mixed memories from South Africa four years ago when he was hailed as a hero after scoring the winner against the USA in the last 16, but his last-ditch penalty miss in the quarter-final defeat by Uruguay meant his tournament ended on a sour note.

Much-travelled at club level, Gyan has played in Italy (with Udinese), France (with Rennes) and England (with Sunderland). In 2011 he left the north-east to move to the United Arab Emirates and has since won two league titles with his club, Al Ain.

USA

Football may not be as popular as some other sports in the United States, but American 'soccer' fans have every reason to be proud of their national team. This, after all, will be the USA's seventh consecutive appearance at the World Cup finals – a record that many football-loving nations would be happy to claim for their own.

More significantly, perhaps, the USA will travel to Brazil in tremendous form. Not only did they comfortably win their CONCACAF final qualifying group, finishing four points clear of second-placed Costa Rica, but they also enjoyed a magnificent 12-match winning run in 2013 which was kicked off by a sensational 4-3 friendly victory over Germany in Washington.

> **"I had a feeling in my stomach we'd get Germany. It's one of the most difficult groups in the whole draw."**
> USA coach
> Jurgen Klinsmann

That result will have delighted USA boss Jurgen Klinsmann, who famously won the World Cup with Germany in 1990 before leading his country to the semi-finals as hosts in 2006. He will not expect to replicate those achievements with the USA, but the former Tottenham striker has created a well-organised, physically fit side which also carries a goal threat.

In Brazil, Klinsmann will mainly rely on a core of experienced players who include Everton goalkeeper Tim Howard, a pair of tireless midfielders in Besiktas' Jermaine Jones and Toronto's Michael Bradley, and support strikers Landon Donovan and Clint Dempsey. The latter duo will look to get forward as often as possible alongside burly target man Jozy Altidore, who has struggled with Sunderland in the Premier League but was the USA's top scorer in qualification with five goals.

The USA reached the second round at the last World Cup in South Africa after pipping England to first place in their group, and Klinsmann will be disappointed not to do at least as well this summer.

USA AT THE WORLD CUP

• The USA competed at the first World Cup in Uruguay in 1930, reaching the last four after 3-0 victories over Belgium and Paraguay. In the second of these matches Bert Patanaude scored all his team's goals to claim the very first hat-trick at the finals. In the semi-finals, though, the USA were outclassed by Argentina, losing 6-1.

• **In 1950 the USA pulled off arguably the greatest ever surprise in World Cup history, beating England 1-0 in Belo Horizonte, Brazil, thanks to a headed goal by Haitian-born striker Joe Gaetjens.**

• The USA hosted the tournament in 1994 and reached the knockout stage for the first time since 1930. In the last 16 they ran eventual winners Brazil close, but couldn't take advantage when their opponents went down to 10 men and eventually lost 1-0.

• **The USA again made it to the last 16 in 2010 in South Africa, losing 2-1 to Ghana after extra-time. Along the way they shocked England once more, holding them to a 1-1 draw in their first match.**

PREVIOUS TOURNAMENTS

1930 Third place	1966 Did not qualify	1994 Round 2
1934 Round 1	1970 Did not qualify	1998 Round 1
1938 Withdrew	1974 Did not qualify	2002 Quarter-finals
1950 Round 1	1978 Did not qualify	2006 Round 1
1954 Did not qualify	1982 Did not qualify	2010 Round 2
1958 Did not qualify	1986 Did not qualify	
1962 Did not qualify	1990 Round 1	

KEY PLAYER

CLINT DEMPSEY

A clever player who can operate equally effectively as an attacking midfielder or as a withdrawn striker, USA captain Clint Dempsey is his country's second ever highest scorer with nearly 40 goals to his name. Extremely experienced, Dempsey represented the US at both the 2006 and 2010 World Cups, famously notching the equaliser against England in the second of these tournaments in South Africa.

After starting out with New England Revolution in the MLS, Texas-born Dempsey joined Fulham in 2007. He spent five successful seasons in west London, becoming the Cottagers' all-time leading Premier League goalscorer and helping them reach the inaugural Europa League final in 2010 – in the process making history as the first American to play in a major European final.

Dempsey moved to Tottenham in a £6 million deal in 2012, but only spent a year there before returning to his homeland to play for Seattle Sounders.

BELGIUM

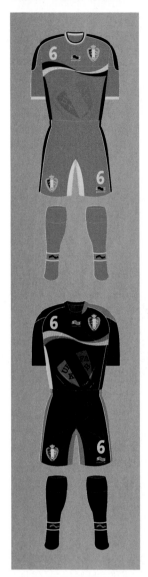

Despite having failed to qualify for the past two World Cups, Belgium are tipped by many pundits to do extremely well in Brazil. Little wonder, really, when you consider that the Red Devils have a squad full of exciting young talents, many of them playing in the Premier League, and showed their class by qualifying for this summer's tournament in fine style.

Belgium finished an impressive nine points ahead of Croatia in their group – a margin only matched by the Netherlands in the European qualifying section. The foundation of their success was a strong defence which conceded a paltry four goals. Highly-rated goalkeeper Thibaut Courtois, on loan for the past two seasons from Chelsea to Atletico Madrid, is a key component of Belgium's rearguard and rarely makes a mistake.

In front of him, meanwhile, captain Vincent Kompany and Arsenal's Thomas Vermaelen are a pair of rock-solid central defenders, while extra defensive ballast is provided by another Premier League duo – tough-tackling holding midfielders Marouane Fellaini and Moussa Dembele.

With such a strong backline, Belgium often only need one goal to win a game and they have the attacking players to more than meet that requirement. In coach Marc Wilmots's 4-2-3-1 formation Chelsea's sublimely skilled Eden Hazard is charged with performing the prime creative role, but he has excellent support from the likes of Wolfsburg's Kevin de Bruyne, Everton star Kevin Mirallas and Zenit Saint Petersburg's Axel Witsal.

Wilmots will have to make a big decision about who plays as the solitary striker. Aston Villa's Christian Benteke got the nod for most of the qualifiers, but the claims of rising star Romelu Lukaku will be difficult to ignore after an impressive season on loan at Everton from Chelsea.

> **"Our group is interesting but tricky, because there is no hiding place for us. Next round is a must."**
>
> Belgium captain Vincent Kompany

THE GAFFER: MARC WILMOTS

Appointed Belgium manager in May 2012 after previously having served as the team's assistant coach, Marc Wilmots has overseen the best run of results the Red Devils have enjoyed for many years. While he has been fortunate in inheriting the finest crop of players Belgium have produced for at least three decades, he also deserves credit for making the most of some disparate talents and merging them into a cohesive unit. He is, though, reluctant to talk up his team, saying, "We can only talk about a golden generation once these players have made some good results and won some trophies."

Wilmots has also encouraged Belgium to play in a swift counter-attacking manner, which very much mirrors his own style as a midfielder with Standard Liege and Schalke. With the latter outfit Wilmots won the UEFA Cup in 1997, scoring the trophy-clinching penalty in a shoot-out against Inter Milan. At international level, he represented Belgium at four World Cups between 1990 and 2002, scoring a total of five goals – a record for his country at the finals.

After hanging up his boots, Wilmots briefly moved into politics with the Reformist Movement and was elected to the Belgian Senate in 2003.

KEY PLAYER

EDEN HAZARD

A creative midfielder who has been compared to Argentine genius Lionel Messi, Eden Hazard could inspire Belgium to great things at this summer's World Cup.

Whether he plays on the flank or in a more central area, the Chelsea man is always a threat, never happier than when he uses his superb close ball skills to take on defenders in tight situations. He can score spectacular goals, too, as he has demonstrated on a number of occasions since joining the Londoners from Lille for £32 million in May 2012. Twice voted French Player of the Year, Hazard was also named in the PFA Team of the Year in his first season at Stamford Bridge, despite an embarrassing incident at Swansea when he was sent off for kicking the ball out of the grasp of a ball boy.

Hazard was first capped by Belgium in 2008 when aged just 17, but hasn't always managed to reproduce his brilliant club form at international level. However, if he is at his best in Brazil he could well be one of the brightest stars of the tournament.

ONE TO WATCH: ROMELU LUKAKU

For most of Belgium's World Cup qualifying campaign Romelu Lukaku had to be content with a place on the Red Devils' bench. However, given a rare start away to Croatia he seized the opportunity with relish, scoring both his country's goals in a 2-1 win to guarantee Belgium's passage to Brazil.

More than the goals, though, the way Lukaku terrorised the Croatian defence with his pace, power and technical ability gave coach Marc Wilmots much food for thought. He will surely be tempted to give the former Anderlecht striker more chances in the summer, especially as Lukaku has impressed out on loan from his parent club, Chelsea.

At West Bromwich Albion during the 2012/13 season Lukaku was sensational, netting 17 goals to finish as the sixth top scorer in the Premier League. The following campaign he starred again for Everton, scoring the winner on his debut at West Ham and then finding the target on a regular basis as the season continued.

Indeed, his form was so striking few could understand why Blues boss Jose Mourinho allowed him to leave Stamford Bridge in the first place.

TACTICS BOARD

WARNING! HAZARD

Belgium generally line up in an attractive 4-2-3-1 formation that gives their gifted offensive players freedom to express themselves.

Eden Hazard, who starts on the left side of attack but loves to get involved centrally in the build-up play, is a key figure for the Red Devils. Belgium prefer to play on the counter-attack, exploiting the raw pace of their lone striker – either Romelu Lukaku or Christian Benteke – but when the opposition drops deep Hazard is the man most likely to unlock a tight defence. Alongside him, Tintin-lookalike Kevin de Bruyne is a direct, hard-running player who usually operates in the middle, while Everton's Kevin Mirallas and Zenit Saint Petersburg's Axel Witsal are good options on the right.

Behind this attacking quartet, Tottenham's Moussa Dembele and Manchester United's Marouane Fellaini are physically imposing defensive midfielders who provide extra protection for a well-drilled defence marshalled by captain Vincent Kompany.

BELGIUM AT THE WORLD CUP

• Along with France, Romania and Yugoslavia, Belgium were one of just four European countries to appear at the first World Cup in Uruguay. The Red Devils, though, didn't have much to write home about after failing to score a single goal in defeats to the USA (3-0) and Paraguay (1-0).

• Belgium played in the first of just two 4-4 draws in World Cup history in 1954, sharing eight goals with England in Basel, Switzerland. The Belgians were indebted to Portsmouth's Jimmy Dickinson who rounded off the scoring with a headed own goal.

• Remarkably, the Belgians had to wait until 1970 before recording their first ever victory at the finals, a 3-0 defeat of minnows El Salvador. However, after losing 4-1 to the Soviet Union and 1-0 to hosts Mexico they were soon packing their bags for home.

• In the opening match of the 1982 tournament in Spain, a single goal by Erwin Vandenbergh gave Belgium a surprise victory over reigning champions Argentina. For the first time the Red Devils progressed to the second round, where they lost both pool games to Poland and the Soviet Union.

• Belgium's best ever showing at the World Cup came in 1986 in Mexico, when they came fourth. In the last

Jan Ceulemans bursts forward against the Soviet Union in 1986

16 they saw off the Soviet Union in a 4-3 thriller, despite conceding a hat-trick to Igor Belanov. They then beat Spain on penalties before losing 2-0 to a Diego Maradona-inspired Argentina in the semi-finals. The Belgians' star man was skilful midfielder Enzo Scifo who was named as the best young player at the tournament.

• At the 1990 finals in Italy, Belgium were eliminated in the last 16 by one of the latest goals in World Cup history when England's David Platt struck a superb volley on the turn in the last minute of extra-time.

• Four years later Belgian claimed a famous 1-0 win over neighbours the Netherlands in the group stage, future Newcastle defender Philippe Albert grabbing the winner. In the second round, though, the Red Devils were beaten 3-2 by Germany in Chicago. There was some consolation, however, for Belgium's Michel Preud'homme, who was named as the tournament's best goalkeeper.

• Belgium qualified for a sixth consecutive World Cup in 2002. Again they went out in the second round, losing a tight game 2-0 to eventual winners Brazil.

PREVIOUS TOURNAMENTS

1930 Round 1	1966 Did not qualify	1994 Round 2
1934 Round 1	1970 Round 1	1998 Round 1
1938 Round 1	1974 Did not qualify	2002 Round 2
1950 Withdrew	1978 Did not qualify	2006 Did not qualify
1954 Round 1	1982 Round 2	2010 Did not qualify
1958 Did not qualify	1986 Fourth place	
1962 Did not qualify	1990 Round 2	

ALGERIA

Of all the countries heading to Brazil, Algeria are among the luckiest. Drawn against African Nations Cup runners-up Burkina Faso in the play-offs the Desert Foxes, or Les Fennecs as they are known by their fans, only sneaked through on the away goals rule. The Algerians, though, won't care about their slightly fortunate qualification; instead, they will simply be proud to be the only north African nation at the finals.

Algeria's passage to Brazil was largely built on their incredible home form: of their last 20 games played at their base at the Stade Mustapha Tchaker in Blida they have won 17 and drawn three. Fittingly, then, that's where they booked their place in South America with a 1-0 win over Burkina Faso in the second leg, captain and former Rangers star Majid Bougherra grabbing the vital goal just after the half-time interval.

For Bosnian coach Vahid Halilhodzic it was the second time he had led a team to World Cup qualification, having previously achieved the same feat with Ivory Coast before being sacked just four months ahead of the 2010 finals. Given that distressing experience, he could be forgiven for counting down the days to the big kick-off in Brazil rather nervously.

A flexible coach who deploys different formations depending on the opposition, Valilhodzic has created a compact team that concedes few goals and has good attacking potential. Valencia winger Sofiane Feghouli is Algeria's most creative player and the side also boasts a couple of dangerous strikers in Dinamo Zagreb's El Arbi Hillel Soudani and Sporting Lisbon's Islam Slimani, his country's top scorer in qualification with five goals.

Algeria will be hoping to match or better their showing at the last World Cup when they held England to a 0-0 draw, and they should pick up points in a competitive-looking group.

> **"We will certainly not go to Brazil for sightseeing, but to represent Algeria in a good light."**
>
> Algeria coach
> Vahid Halilhodzic

ALGERIA AT THE WORLD CUP

• Algeria pulled off one of the biggest shocks at the World Cup in 1982 when, in their first ever match at the finals, they beat West Germany 2-1. The north Africans also defeated Chile 3-2 and seemed set for a place in the second round, but the following day the Germans beat Austria 1-0, a result which ensured that both countries would progress out of their group at the expense of Algeria on goal difference.

• **Outraged, the Algerians protested that West Germany and Austria had colluded to produce an outcome that suited both teams. FIFA dismissed Algeria's complaints although it did rule that the final two matches in a group should be played at the same time at future tournaments.**

• Algeria didn't give their fans much to cheer at their last appearance at the finals in 2010. After a 1-0 defeat to Slovenia, the north Africans surprisingly held England to a 0-0 draw in Cape Town but their hopes of making it through to the knockout stages for the first time were dashed when they lost 1-0 to the USA in their final group match.

PREVIOUS TOURNAMENTS

1930 Did not enter	1966 Withdrew	1994 Did not qualify
1934 Did not enter	1970 Did not qualify	1998 Did not qualify
1938 Did not enter	1974 Did not qualify	2002 Did not qualify
1950 Did not enter	1978 Did not qualify	2006 Did not qualify
1954 Did not enter	1982 Round 1	2010 Round 1
1958 Did not enter	1986 Round 1	
1962 Did not qualify	1990 Did not qualify	

KEY PLAYER

SOFIANE FEGHOULI

A fast, tricky winger who loves to take on and bamboozle defenders, Valencia's Sofiane Feghouli is the Algerian player most likely to shine on the big stage at this summer's World Cup.

Born in Paris in 1989, Feghouli represented France at youth and Under-21 level before committing his international future to Algeria, his parents' homeland, in 2011. The following year he made his debut for the north Africans, scoring against Gambia, although his most important strike for his nation came in the two-legged World Cup play-off against Burkina Faso which Algeria won on the away goals rule.

After originally being rejected by Paris Saint-Germain, Feghouli started his club career with Grenoble, where he was dubbed 'the new Zidane'. Such high praise alerted bigger clubs to his many talents, and in 2010 he was snapped up by Valencia.

After a difficult start to his La Liga career, his exciting wing-play has since made him a firm favourite at the Mestalla.

RUSSIA

As host nation for the 2018 World Cup, Russia will hope that a good showing in Brazil will help to build up enthusiasm for the tournament back home when the finals return to Europe in four years' time. However, a glance at the record books reveals little to encourage the Russians, who have just one quarter-final appearance to their name since coming fourth way back at the 1966 World Cup in England.

At least Russia have a highly respected coach in charge of their squad, in the form of former England manager Fabio Capello. Mind you, the Italian can't have enjoyed his last World Cup experience very much, as the Three Lions crashed out in spectacular style in the last 16, on the wrong end of a 4-1 thrashing against Germany after failing to impress in their three group games.

> "It's a good group, the draw is not so bad. I'm happy!"
> Russia coach Fabio Capello

After resigning from the England job in 2012, Capello, you feel, will have a point to prove and the signs are that he will adopt a generally cautious approach in an effort to make his side difficult to

beat. Russia, then, are likely to line up in a defensive 4-1-4-1 formation, with captain Igor Denisov of Dynamo Moscow patrolling the area in front of a compact back four which, along with goalkeeper Igor Akinfeev, will largely be drawn from the ranks of CSKA Moscow.

Building from this solid base, Russia will attempt to launch swift counter-attacks by quickly transferring the ball from the back to talented central midfielders, Roman Shirokov and Viktor Fayzulin, both of Zenit Saint Petersburg. They, in turn, will look to feed their club team-mate, striker Aleksandr Kerzhakov, who has excellent movement and a respectable one-in-three strike rate in internationals.

Although Russia's poor track record at the World Cup does not inspire confidence, they have been given a decent draw and have every chance of making a first appearance in the last 16 since 1986.

RUSSIA AT THE WORLD CUP

• Russia's best showing at the World Cup came in 1966 in England when, in their former guise as the Soviet Union, they reached the semi-finals. However, despite the best efforts of their legendary goalkeeper Lev Yashin, they were beaten 2-1 by West Germany at Everton's Goodison Park.

• **At the 1994 World Cup in the USA Russian striker Oleg Salenko set a new individual record for the finals when he scored five goals in a 6-1 hammering of Cameroon. The result didn't do his team much good, though, as after previous defeats to Brazil and Sweden, the Russians had already been eliminated from the competition.**

• Russia last appeared at the finals in 2002, but it was a far from happy experience. A 2-0 win over Tunisia represented a good start but the Russians then lost consecutive matches to co-hosts Japan and Belgium to end their interest in the tournament, the first of these defeats sparking violent riots back in Moscow by thousands of football hooligans which left two dead and 73 people injured.

PREVIOUS TOURNAMENTS

1930 Did not enter	1966 Fourth place	1994 Round 1
1934 Did not enter	1970 Quarter-finals	1998 Did not qualify
1938 Did not enter	1974 Disqualified	2002 Round 1
1950 Did not enter	1978 Did not qualify	2006 Did not qualify
1954 Did not enter	1982 Round 2	2010 Did not qualify
1958 Quarter-finals	1986 Round 2	
1962 Quarter-finals	1990 Round 1	

KEY PLAYER

ROMAN SHIROKOV

Roman Shirokov is an experienced midfielder who likes to direct play for his team while occasionally getting forward to support his strikers. The Zenit Saint Petersburg veteran can also play at centre-back, a role he performed capably in his club's 2-0 defeat of Rangers in the 2008 UEFA Cup final.

Shirokov made his international debut in a friendly against Romania in 2008, the same year he joined Zenit from FC Khimki. He featured briefly at the Euro 2008 Championships and played in all three of Russia's games at Euro 2012, scoring in the 4-1 rout of the Czech Republic.

A three-time Russian league title winner with Zenit, Shirokov is an outspoken character who enjoys baiting the opposition. After a victory over Spartak Moscow in 2011 he crowed, "I congratulate pigs for deserved loss" while he also upset Slovakian fans by describing their country as "a collective farm" before a Euro 2012 qualifier.

SOUTH KOREA

South Korea will make their eighth consecutive appearance at the finals in Brazil this summer – easily the best record of any Asian nation. Urged on by their fanatical red T-shirted fans when they co-hosted the tournament in 2002, the Koreans famously reached the semi-finals, but few would bet on them doing anywhere near as well this time round.

Despite their excellent past record, South Korea rather limped through the qualifying stages. Indeed, after losing twice to group winners Iran, they only booked their place in South America on goal difference ahead of Uzbekistan. An uninspiring campaign led to a change in manager with Hong Myung-Bo, the heroic captain of the 2002 legends, taking over as coach in June 2013.

> **"People may think it's an easy group, but it's not true."**
> South Korea coach
> Hong Myung-Bo

Hong will seek to implant the values of hard work, good organisation and boundless enthusiasm that have previously served South Korea so well. He will be helped in this enterprise by a core of players who have vital experience in European football, including skipper Lee Chung-Yong of Bolton, Cardiff's attacking midfielder Kim Bo-Kyung and £6 million midfielder Ki Sung-Yueng, who spent the 2013/14 season on loan at Sunderland from Swansea. There may even be a place for Park Chu-Young, a striker on Arsenal's books who has been spotted in his natural habitat about as often as the Loch Ness Monster. Now on loan at Watford, he was South Korea's leading scorer in qualification with six goals.

Given their mediocre recent form and their lack of star quality, it's difficult to see South Korea replicating their experience of South Africa in 2010, when they reached the second round. And if they do go out early don't expect any sympathy from the world's football commentators – after all, the South Korean squad could include as many as six 'Kims' and five 'Lees'!

SOUTH KOREA AT THE WORLD CUP

• South Korea's first match at the World Cup in 1954 in Switzerland was one to forget, as they were crushed 9-0 by Hungary – at the time the heaviest defeat in the tournament's history. They fared better in their second game, though, only losing 7-0 to Turkey!

• Hosting the tournament with Japan in 2002, South Korea at last claimed their first victory at the finals when they beat Poland 2-0. After topping their group, they then sensationally beat Italy in the last 16 thanks to a late goal by Ahn Jung-Hwan. The next day his Italian club, Perugia, announced that Jung-Hwan would not play for them again as he had "ruined" Italian football.

• In the quarter-finals in 2002 South Korea beat Spain on penalties, but their luck ran out in the last four when they lost 1-0 to Germany.

• On their last appearance at the finals in 2010 in South Africa, South Korea reached the second round for a second time but were gunned down by Luis Suarez who scored both Uruguay's goals in his side's 2-1 victory.

PREVIOUS TOURNAMENTS

1930 Did not enter	1966 Did not qualify	1994 Round 1
1934 Did not enter	1970 Did not qualify	1998 Round 1
1938 Did not enter	1974 Did not qualify	2002 Fourth place
1950 Did not enter	1978 Did not qualify	2006 Round 1
1954 Round 1	1982 Did not qualify	2010 Round 2
1958 Entry not accepted	1986 Round 1	
1962 Did not qualify	1990 Round 2	

KEY PLAYER

LEE CHUNG-YONG

An energetic and skilful player who is equally at home in midfield or on the wing, South Korea captain Lee Chung-Yong is a hugely popular figure in his homeland.

First capped against Jordan in 2008, he was his country's standout performer at the World Cup in South Africa two years later, scoring goals against Argentina and Uruguay in the group stage and second round respectively.

The 'Blue Dragon', as his army of South Korean fans call him, started out with FC Seoul before moving to Bolton Wanderers for a bargain £2.2 million in 2009. After a string of impressive displays for the Trotters, he was voted 'Bolton Player of the Year' at the end of his first season.

In July 2011, though, the diminutive South Korean broke his leg in a friendly against Newport County and missed virtually the whole of the campaign. Now fully recovered, he will hope to be firing on all cylinders in Brazil as his country targets qualifying for the knockout phase for the third time.

EDEN HAZARD

Eden Hazard has always seemed destined for football stardom. The game is in his family's blood – both his parents were footballers in Belgium, while his brother Thorgen is also a professional player.

Just like Wayne Rooney and James Milner in the Premier League, Hazard burst onto the scene when he should have still been at school, making his debut for Lille in France's Ligue 1 at just 16. International honours soon followed with a first cap at 17, and it wasn't long before his country's press hailed the skilful starlet as the successor to the greatest Belgian of all, Enzo Scifo.

The accolades and awards have come thick and fast ever since: the first overseas footballer to win France's Young Player of the Year award in 2009, then the first to retain it the following year, a league and cup Double with Lille in 2011, and back-to-back French Player of the Year honours in 2011 and 2012.

Inevitably, Hazard attracted the attention of the giants of European football, with France legend and Real Madrid assistant coach Zinedine Zidane delivering this endorsement. "Eden is technically gifted and very fast. I would take him to Real Madrid with my eyes closed," he said.

After a lengthy battle between several clubs, the Belgian signed for Chelsea in the summer of 2012 for £32 million. Blues owner Roman Abramovich can feel very satisfied with his investment so far.

After helping Chelsea win the Europa League in his first season and earning nominations for the PFA's Player of the Year and Young Player of the Year gongs, Hazard has thrived since the return of Jose Mourinho. He has developed into the club's key playmaker, while at the same time upping his work-rate to fit in with his manager's defensive game plan.

The same height as Lionel Messi, Hazard boasts several similar traits. He terrifies defenders, running directly at them and able to beat them either with a trick or raw pace. He conjures opportunities with either foot and also has an eye for goal, particularly when he cuts in from the left wing to unleash a spectacular long-range effort.

In a Belgium team jam-packed with talent, Hazard stands out as a shining light. His skills, speed and unique ability to create something out of nothing could take his country a long way in Brazil.

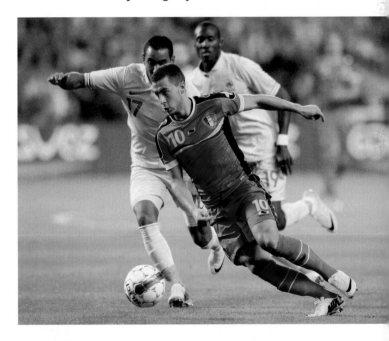

Will Eden Hazard live up to his billing in Belgium as the next Enzo Scifo?

STATS

DOB: 07/01/1991
Country: Belgium
International debut: v Luxembourg,
  19/11/2008
Caps: 42 Goals: 5
World Cup finals appearances: 0
World Cup finals goals: 0

ANDRES INIESTA

What is left for Andres Iniesta to achieve? The brilliant playmaker of the Barcelona and Spain midfields has won almost every title imaginable, at both club and international level. So much so that it has been rare to watch a major final in recent years when Iniesta has not featured.

While Barcelona have long been a force of club football, the rise of Spain to the pinnacle of the international game has been even more impressive after so many years of near misses and underachievement. And Iniesta has been a pivotal figure every step of the way.

Selected in the team of the tournament at Euro 2008, the midfield wizard went one step better at Poland and Ukraine 2012 when he was named the player of the championships as the Spanish defended their European crown. He won no less than three man of the match awards that tournament, including the 4-0 thrashing of Italy in the final.

Sandwiched between the two Euro triumphs, of course, is Iniesta's crowning glory – the World Cup – won thanks to his strike against the Netherlands in the final four years ago with five minutes of extra-time remaining. If that wasn't good enough, he walked off with the man of the match award too. Clearly, this is a player who relishes the big stage.

So what next for the man who has everything? Is it not time to let someone else have a turn? But therein lies the secret ingredient of a player like Iniesta. He is constantly hungry for more: more wins, more goals, more titles, more assists, more trophy celebrations. To play the best and beat the best. As we have seen time and again with Barcelona and Spain.

The challenge for Spain is to become the first country since Brazil in 1962 to win back-to-back World Cups. To do so, they will need a fit and firing Andres Iniesta. A player with quick feet, sublime dribbling skills, ghostly movement and the most intelligent of football brains. A player who has already won one World Cup final and could easily repeat the feat.

Can Andres Iniesta lead Spain to yet more success on the world stage?

STATS

DOB: 11/05/1984
Country: Spain
International debut: v Russia, 27/05/2006
Caps: 94 Goals: 10
World Cup finals appearances: 2006, 2010
(7 apps)
World Cup finals goals: 2

LIONEL MESSI

What more can Lionel Messi do to prove he is the best footballer in the world? The answer is simple: win a World Cup. The reality, of course, is much harder. Such is the extent of the Argentinian's achievements that a whole book would barely do justice to them, let alone a couple of pages. Champions League, La Liga, European Golden Shoe, Club World Cup, Ballon d'Or – you name it, Messi has won it, and often many times over.

There is only one major trophy left for Lionel Messi to win (and we don't mean the Europa League!)

STATS

DOB: 24/06/1987
Country: Argentina
International debut: v Hungary, 17/08/2005
Caps: 78 Goals: 39
World Cup finals appearances: 2006, 2010
(8 apps)
World Cup finals goals: 1

With Argentina, however, while he tasted Olympic gold and won the Under-20 World Cup, the diminutive No.10 has failed to add to his glittering list of honours with the senior side. In eight matches at the World Cup, Messi has scored just once and struggled to reproduce the scintillating performances he turns on for Barcelona on a weekly basis, as Argentina have fallen at the hands of Germany in both the 2006 and 2010 quarter-finals.

More recently, though, and ominously for their rivals, the national side has brought the best out of Messi. In World Cup qualifying, he netted 10 times as Argentina romped to top spot in their group. Those goals ensured he leapt past Diego Maradona and Hernan Crespo in his country's all-time scoring list. Only Gabriel Batistuta has scored more.

At club level, Messi's individual exploits become more impressive by the season. Perhaps most staggering of all was his record in 2013 when he became the first professional footballer in history to score in consecutive matches against every other team in the league (there are 20 teams in La Liga!). Messi, more than any other player, has been the driving force behind Barcelona earning a reputation as the greatest club side of the modern era.

It is no surprise that he was voted the world's best player four years in a row. If he could add a World Cup winner's medal to his already overflowing trophy cabinet, there would be no argument that he sits alongside such luminaries as Pele, Diego Maradona, Zinedine Zidane and Franz Beckenbauer as one of the greatest players ever to have kicked a football. The only debate would surround Messi's position in the pecking order.

NEYMAR

No sooner had the dust settled on Spain's victory at the 2010 World Cup than attention turned to Brazil 2014, and an entire country expecting the Samba boys to lift the trophy for an unprecedented sixth time. One man will carry that pressure more than the rest of his team combined.

Controversially omitted from Brazil's World Cup squad for South Africa at 18 years old, Neymar has been the focal point of the host nation's preparations for this tournament. Instantly recognisable with his outlandish hairstyles, he is blessed with many of the skills which the football world associates with Brazilian football – speed, quick feet, tricks, wonderful control, devastating finishing. So much so that many pundits have likened him to the greatest Brazilian of them all, Pele.

Having joined Santos' youth academy at 11, Neymar remained at the club for a decade, enjoying notable success – and earning a burgeoning reputation – with the highlight being the Copa Libertadores success in 2011. As the Neymar legend grew, a succession of European heavyweight clubs tried to get his signature. Eventually, Barcelona persuaded the striker to leave Brazil when they signed him for £48.6 million in the summer of 2013. By that time, he was a two-time winner of the South American Footballer of the Year award.

Neymar made his international debut in the immediate aftermath of Brazil's disappointing campaign in South Africa, and it quickly became apparent that he would be a pivotal figure for years to come. He needed just 28 minutes to score his first goal against the USA.

At the 2013 Confederations Cup, the dress rehearsal for the 2014 tournament, Neymar didn't disappoint. Not only did he walk away with a winner's medal after scoring in Brazil's 3-0 defeat of Spain in the final but also the Golden Ball as the tournament's best player.

The world is now recognising him for the superstar he is, with former Brazil striker Ronaldo saying in 2012: "Logically, [Lionel] Messi is better right now but Neymar is a great talent who will show the world that he will be number one."

Neymar will carry the hopes of a nation this summer

STATS

DOB: 05/02/1992
Country: Brazil
International debut: v USA, 10/08/2010
Caps: 62 Goals: 40
World Cup finals appearances: 0
World Cup finals goals: 0

MESUT OZIL

For all the fanfare of Gareth Bale's world-record transfer from Tottenham Hotspur to Real Madrid in 2013, it was the move of another player in the opposite direction which might have been the most important deal that summer. Mesut Ozil left the Spanish capital to join Arsenal for almost exactly half the money Madrid had parted with, becoming the most expensive German footballer of all time. Within weeks it was clear he would justify that price tag, and help transform the north London side's fortunes in the process.

It takes more than two players to stop Mesut Ozil

STATS

DOB: 15/10/1988
Country: Germany
International debut: v Norway, 11/02/2009
Caps: 52 Goals: 17
World Cup finals appearances: 2010 (7 apps)
World Cup finals goals: 1

A third-generation Turkish-German, Ozil has been making headlines ever since he inspired Germany to victory in the 2009 European Under-21 Championships. Scoring a goal and setting up two others in the 4-0 rout of old enemy England in the final would have done nothing to harm his popularity.

A year later, German fans were singing his praises once more as Ozil played a pivotal role in his country's run to the World Cup semi-finals and was one of 10 players nominated for the Golden Ball as the tournament's best player. If any further proof were needed that he was a natural on the big stage, he was named on the shortlist for the best player at Euro 2012 after another eye-catching few weeks.

An attacking midfielder blessed with extraordinary vision, Ozil can make a goal with a flick of the boot or a perfectly weighted pass. He led La Liga in assists when Madrid won the title in 2012 and flourishes in his role as chief creator for Arsenal. Far from being just a provider, he scores plenty of goals too and was the top scorer in Germany's World Cup qualification campaign, finding the net seven times.

In the past four major tournaments, the richly talented German team have reached three semi-finals and one final, but are yet to get their hands on the trophy. With Ozil pulling the strings in Brazil, that may be about to change.

FRANCK RIBERY

Ask any football fan to name the world's finest footballer and the answer will almost invariably be one of two options: Lionel Messi or Cristiano Ronaldo. In 2013, however, a third name entered the mix: Franck Ribery. To his enormous credit, the flying Frenchman made people think again about the best player on the planet, after inspiring Bayern Munich to a glory-filled year.

With Ribery pulling the strings, the German side picked up practically every trophy on offer – the domestic league and cup Double, then the Champions League, before seeing off Chelsea in the UEFA Super Cup for good measure.

Playing on his favoured left wing, from where he frequently cuts inside onto his feared right foot, Ribery was the inspiration behind Bayern's all-conquering campaign. His contribution was duly recognised when he won UEFA's award for the best player in Europe and finished third in the World Player of the Year award.

In truth, the Frenchman had been tipped for such glittering honours ever since he exploded onto the international scene at the 2006 World Cup. Just one month after his debut for his country, aged only 23, he played a pivotal part in France's run to the final in Germany, delivering a memorable performance, and also scoring, in a 3-1 win over Spain in the last 16. That was the last time the Spanish have failed to win a major tournament.

During that World Cup Ribery was mentored by none other than Zinedine Zidane, who described the young player as the "jewel of French football". And in the wake of their loss to Italy in the final, the title of France's talisman was passed from Zidane to Ribery.

The French have encountered many well-documented mishaps since then, and neither the team nor its star player have always lived up to expectation. But things could be different in 2014. Ribery goes to Brazil in the form of his career and desperate to take his country one step further than 2006.

Franck Ribery will be hoping to repeat his World Cup heroics of 2006 in Brazil

STATS

DOB: 07/04/1983
Country: France
International debut: v Mexico, 27/05/2006
Caps: 80 Goals: 16
World Cup finals appearances: 2006, 2010
(10 apps)
World Cup finals goals: 1

CRISTIANO RONALDO

If any confirmation were needed about Cristiano Ronaldo's standing as a superstar of the modern game, he provided an emphatic answer in last November's do-or-die play-off against Sweden.

The match was billed as a duel between Ronaldo and another football giant, Zlatan Ibrahimovic, and so it proved as the pair scored all six goals over two legs. Luckily for Portugal, Ronaldo bagged four of them, propelling his country to the 2014 World Cup almost singlehandedly, and leaving the Swedes to think about how to fill their summer holidays.

Those who witnessed his stunning hat-trick in Stockholm will never forget it. It was Ronaldo's fifth treble of the 2013/14 season (remember, this was only November). The haul drew him level with Pauleta as Portugal's leading all-time scorer on 47 goals.

There was no shortage of praise for the Portuguese captain after the match. Former England striker Gary Lineker said: "I don't care how many trophies [Franck] Ribery has won, the best player is the best player. And this year that is undisputedly Cristiano Ronaldo." Even FIFA president Sepp Blatter was moved to tweet: "Fantastic performance by Ronaldo."

Yet this was no one-off. The point about Ronaldo is he delivers these performances on a scarily regular basis. The goals against Sweden took his total scoring tally for the calendar year to 66 from 55 games. He is devastatingly quick – either with the ball or without it, imperious in the air, blessed with a ferocious shot with either foot and a threat from any free-kick within 40 yards of goal.

Ronaldo has been the heartbeat of every team he plays for: Manchester United, Portugal, Real Madrid – regardless of the world-record signing of Gareth Bale. Since moving to Madrid in 2009, he has torn up the record books and was rewarded with the World Player of the Year award in January 2014.

Portugal have been revitalised in major tournaments with Ronaldo, coming within a whisker of winning Euro 2004 and reaching two other semi-finals. Such is his importance to his country that it is unlikely they would even be going to Brazil were Ronaldo not in the team. With him, they can dream of winning it.

The 2014 World Cup could be all about Cristiano Ronaldo

STATS

DOB: 05/02/1985
Country: Portugal
International debut: v Kazakhstan, 20/08/2003
Caps: 109 Goals: 47
World Cup finals appearances: 2006, 2010
(10 apps)
World Cup finals goals: 2

WAYNE ROONEY

The image of a teenage Wayne Rooney tearing past the best defenders in Europe, game after game, lives long in the hearts and minds of England fans. It was Euro 2004, a fitting occasion for the 18-year-old striker to announce his presence on the international stage.

A breathtaking performance against France was followed by a brace of goals against both Switzerland and Croatia, which propelled Sven-Goran Eriksson's team through the group stages. Even though his tournament and – many would argue – England's hopes were ended by injury in the quarter-final against host nation Portugal, Rooney had already done enough to be named in the team of the championships.

Ten years on, he has picked up a swag of honours for Manchester United and is on the verge of replacing Bobby Charlton as the club's all-time leading goalscorer. Tellingly, he is also closing in on Charlton's record of 49 goals for England, a mythical number which the likes of Gary Lineker, Alan Shearer and Michael Owen have threatened – but never quite managed – to overhaul.

Yet in international tournaments, Rooney has never come close to the heights of Portugal 2004. He has been blighted by misfortune (some his own doing), be it the 2006 World Cup which was ruined by a pre-tournament injury, then a red card for stamping on Portugal's Ricardo Carvalho, or the 2012 European Championships where he sat out the opening two games through suspension.

Nevertheless, Rooney remains his country's talisman, the one player more than any other who could end England's much-publicised wait for international glory. (For the record, it's 48 years now.) He blossomed in qualifying once again, scoring seven goals to take his overall tally in World Cup qualifiers to 16 from 22 matches. Manager Roy Hodgson appears to have settled on a formation that brings the best out of his star man, playing him just off the main striker, the same role that Rooney thrives on behind Robin van Persie at Old Trafford.

In June 2013, Rooney scored a stunning goal in a 2-2 draw with Brazil at the Maracana. England will be relying on more of the same, and a repeat of his Portugal heroics, when they return to South America.

England will hope for more strikes like this from Wayne Rooney – and more opponents ducking out of the way!

STATS

DOB: 24/10/1985
Country: England
International debut: v Australia, 12/02/2003
Caps: 88 Goals: 38
World Cup finals appearances: 2006, 2010
(8 apps)
World Cup finals goals: 0

LUIS SUAREZ

Controversy has never been far from Luis Suarez's side during his career. The supremely skilled Liverpool striker has often attracted attention for the wrong reasons, be it a racism row with Manchester United's Patrice Evra or a 10-match ban for biting Chelsea defender Branislav Ivanovic.

His debut appearance at the World Cup in South Africa was no different. In Uruguay's quarter-final against Ghana, with the scores tied at 1-1, Suarez deliberately handled a goal-bound header in the final minute of extra-time. He was promptly sent off but lingered on the sidelines long enough to celebrate Asamoah Gyan missing the penalty that would have sent the Ghanaians into the semi-finals. Uruguay won the ensuing shoot-out, breaking the hearts of the whole of Africa.

He may polarise opinion but he is also one of the most talented players on the planet. As he proved in South Africa where Suarez emerged as one of the stars of the World Cup, scoring three goals in Uruguay's charge to the semi-finals.

In recent years, his talents have been on show on a weekly basis for Liverpool, as Suarez has lit up the Premier League with his breathtaking dribbling, lethal finishing and, in 2013/14, a formidable partnership with England striker Daniel Sturridge. He finished runner-up behind Gareth Bale in the PFA Players' Player of the Year award in 2013, with many suggesting he would have won were it not for his controversial reputation.

Together with Paris Saint-Germain superstar Edinson Cavani and 2010 World Cup player of the tournament Diego Forlan, Suarez is part of one of the most devastating strikeforces in international football. He is no less prolific in Uruguay colours than he is for Liverpool. The forward averages nearly a goal every other game in World Cup qualifiers and, in 2013, surpassed Forlan as his country's all-time leading scorer.

On top of that, Suarez is a proven performer on the big stage. In addition to his exploits in South Africa, he was named the player of the tournament in the 2011 Copa America, his four goals pivotal to Uruguay lifting the trophy. Don't be surprised if he rises to the occasion in Brazil once again.

If he has his way, Luis Suarez will leave his opponents holding their heads in their hands

STATS

DOB: 24/01/1987
Country: Uruguay
International debut: v Colombia, 08/02/2007
Caps: 72 Goals: 35
World Cup finals appearances: 2010 (6 apps)
World Cup finals goals: 3

YAYA TOURE

Pele once famously predicted that an African nation would win the World Cup before the year 2000. Fourteen years on, we are still waiting for a country from that continent to get past the quarter-finals, but if Yaya Toure has anything to do with it, the Brazilian great may finally be proved right – albeit a little later than anticipated.

A player blessed with the rare combination of silky skills and raw power, Toure will be carrying the hopes of the Ivory Coast on his giant shoulders in Brazil. The fact that he is the standout player in a team which boasts the talents of Didier Drogba, Salomon Kalou and Cheick Tiote is testament alone to Toure's ability. That ability was rewarded in 2011, 2012 and 2013 when he was named Africa's Footballer of the Year, the first time a midfielder had won the award since Morocco's Mustapha Hadji back in 1998.

Toure, whose brother Kolo is another key member of the Ivory Coast side, made his name at Barcelona, winning a Champions League medal in 2009 as the Catalans claimed an historic six trophies in the same calendar year. A versatile box-to-box midfielder who can make a goal-saving tackle in his own box one minute, then curl in a 25-yard free-kick the next, he was exactly the type of player Manchester City were looking for in 2010.

Within a year of his arrival at the Etihad Stadium, Toure had an FA Cup winner's medal and, 12 months later, he was a key cog in City's first league title since 1968. He also has an invaluable knack of scoring on the big occasion, such as the winner against bitter rivals Manchester United in the FA Cup semi-final and the only goal in the final a few weeks later.

There is no bigger occasion than a World Cup, and the whole of the Ivory Coast – and maybe even Pele too – will be hoping Toure can deliver once more.

Yaya Toure and his team-mates will be celebrating again if they reach the knockout stages for the first time

STATS

DOB: 13/05/1983
Country: Ivory Coast
International debut: v Egypt, 20/06/2004
Caps: 57 Goals: 14
World Cup finals appearances: 2006, 2010
(6 apps)
World Cup finals goals: 1

ROBIN VAN PERSIE

Robin van Persie will hope it is a case of third time lucky when he captains the Netherlands in their bid for glory in Brazil. After getting his first taste of the World Cup in Germany in 2006 – and scoring an unforgettable free-kick against the Ivory Coast – then the agony of the extra-time defeat to Spain in the 2010 final, the Dutch skipper is aiming to go one better in what is his third, and almost certainly last, World Cup.

To do so, the Netherlands will need a prolific and proven goalscorer. And in Van Persie they have that man.

The striker with the razor-sharp left foot is one of the greatest goalscorers in the history of the Premier League. As he has got older, so he has scored more and more. In 2011, he finished third in the league's scoring chart before leading the way the following season – his last at Arsenal. In the 2012/13 season, the Dutchman's strike rate improved again at Manchester United, his 30 goals playing a major part in his new club's title success.

Anything but a one-trick pony, his goals come in a variety of ways: he can find the net with a tap-in, an over-the-shoulder volley or a smouldering drive from outside the box.

Van Persie has been no less prolific when wearing the famous orange colours of his national team. A hat-trick in the 8-1 thrashing of Hungary in 2013 was the highlight of a wonderful World Cup qualifying campaign in which the captain scored 11 goals, the most by any European player. With those three strikes in Amsterdam Van Persie became the Netherlands' all-time leading goalscorer. When you consider he is now above the likes of Van Nistelrooy, Bergkamp and Kluivert, that feat is even more impressive.

In 1978, the Dutch – without the talents of Johan Cruyff – came within a whisker of becoming the first European country to win the World Cup in South America, only to be denied by Argentina in the final. Now, with Van Persie leading the line, they may be poised to go one step further than that glorious team of the '70s.

Prolific striker Robin van Persie is the Netherlands' all-time leading goalscorer

STATS

DOB: 06/08/1983
Country: Netherlands
International debut: v Romania, 04/06/2005
Caps: 81 Goals: 41
World Cup finals appearances: 2006, 2010
(11 apps)
World Cup finals goals: 2

WORLD CUP HISTORY

The idea of a world football championship was first raised at FIFA's inaugural meeting in Paris in 1904, but only really gained momentum in the 1920s. A proposal to hold a World Cup tournament was agreed in 1928 in Amsterdam, with Uruguay's bid to act as the host nation being accepted the following year. Since then the World Cup finals have been played 19 times, and eight nations have gone on to lift one of the two trophies (Brazil got to keep the first after winning their third tournament in 1970, although it was subsequently stolen and never seen again!).

1930, URUGUAY

Of the 13 countries who arrived in Montevideo in July 1930 only four made the three week boat journey from Europe. Among the absentees were the four Home Nations, who had resigned from FIFA following an argument about payments to amateur players. Germany, Spain and Italy also stayed at home, leaving just France, Belgium, Romania and Yugoslavia to fly the flag for Europe.

Of that quartet only Yugoslavia won their group, after victories against Brazil and Bolivia, to reach the semi-final where they were duly crushed 6-1 by the hosts. The next day, Argentina beat the USA by the same score to join Uruguay in the final.

Although Uruguay had the advantage of playing at home, thousands of Argentinian fans made the journey across the River Plate to support their team. The recently constructed Centenary Stadium in Montevideo was packed with 93,000 fans two hours before kick-off, while behind the scenes the teams argued about which ball to use. Eventually FIFA settled the dispute by ruling that the two countries could use their preferred ball for a half each.

The original World Cup, the Jules Rimet Trophy

Playing with their opponents' ball, Uruguay took an early lead, but Argentina hit back with two goals before half-time to stun the home fans into silence. The hosts, though, dominated after the break and soon equalised through inside-forward Pedro Cea. Ten minutes later left-winger Santos Iriarte restored Uruguay's lead before centre-forward Hector Castro wrapped up his side's victory in the closing seconds.

As Uruguay captain Jose Nasazzi was presented with the gold cup by FIFA President Jules Rimet, motor horns blared in the streets of Montevideo while the ships sounded their sirens in the port. Despite the disappointing turnout from Europe, the first World Cup had been a huge success.

1934, ITALY

By 1934 the World Cup was already starting to expand. No fewer than 32 countries entered the qualifying competition, with half of that number reaching the finals in Italy. For the only time in the history of the tournament the holders, Uruguay, still bitter about being snubbed by the main European powers four years earlier, declined to defend their trophy. Again, the Home Nations stayed away, the FA's dismissive attitude towards the World Cup being summed up by committee member Charles Sutcliffe, who said: "The national associations of England, Scotland, Wales and Ireland have quite enough to do in their own International Championship which seems to me a far better World Championship than the one to be staged in Rome."

This time the tournament was organised on a straight knockout basis, with the two South American representatives, Argentina and Brazil, falling at the first hurdle to Sweden and Spain respectively. Neither of the

The Italian team before the 1934 World Cup final

victors, though, survived the second round, leaving Czechoslovakia, Germany, Austria and Italy to battle it out in the semi-finals. In Milan, the hosts beat the Austrians thanks to a single goal by right-winger Enrique Guaita, one of three former Argentinian internationals in the Italian team. On the same day in Rome, Italian dictator Benito Mussolini watched Czechoslovakia defeat Germany 3-1.

The final, played in front of 45,000 fans at the Stadio Nazionale in Rome, was a tight affair. The Czechs' attractive short-passing game was eventually rewarded 20 minutes from the end when left-winger Antonin Puc scored with a long-range effort after his corner had only partially been cleared. Italy nearly fell two behind when a Czech effort hit the post, but made the most of their luck to equalise through a crazily swerving shot by left-winger Raimundo Orsi, another Argentine, with just eight minutes to play. The match moved into extra-time, centre-forward Angelo Schiavio grabbing the winner for Italy early in the first period after being set up by Guaita.

1938, FRANCE

It was, perhaps, fitting that the third World Cup was held in France in 1938 as two Frenchmen, FIFA President Jules Rimet and Henri Delaunay, Secretary of the French FA, had been instrumental in setting up the competition a decade earlier.

For a second time the tournament followed a knockout pattern, Brazil's incredible 6-5 defeat of Poland the pick of the first round matches. Two of the ties went to replays, Cuba surprisingly beating Romania and

Germany going down to Switzerland despite holding a 2-0 lead at half-time. The Cubans, though, were trounced 8-0 by Sweden in the second round, while Switzerland were eliminated by Hungary, who went on to crush the Swedes 5-1 in the semi-final in Paris. In the other half of the draw, a violent encounter between Brazil and Czechoslovakia produced two broken limbs and three expulsions, and was only settled in the South Americans' favour after a replay. Brazil's World Cup, however, ended when they were beaten 2-1 in the semi-final by holders Italy, who had earlier accounted for the hosts in the second round.

The final in Paris got off to an exciting start, when both teams scored inside the first seven minutes, Pal Titkos cancelling out Gino Colaussi's opener for the Italians. Hungary, though, were finding it difficult to contain Italy's captain and playmaker Giuseppe Meazza, who provided the pass for Silvio Piola

Giuseppe Meazza and Gyorgy Sarosi before the 1938 final

to restore the Azzurri's lead on the quarter-hour mark. Ten minutes before half-time Meazza slotted the ball through to Colaussi, who beat his marker to grab his second goal. To their credit, the Hungarians refused to buckle and reduced the deficit when, following a goalmouth scramble, centre-forward Gyorgy Sarosi poked the ball home midway through the second half. Ten minutes from the end, though, Piola ensured the cup would remain in Italy with a powerful drive that whistled into the Hungarian net.

1950, BRAZIL

Appearing at their first World Cup in Brazil in 1950, England travelled to South America with high hopes that a team containing the attacking talents of Stanley Matthews, Tom Finney and Jackie Milburn would justify their tag as joint favourites alongside the hosts. Even the local press were excited by England's participation, with banner headlines proclaiming 'The Kings of Football Have Arrived'.

Following a routine win over Chile in which Blackpool's Stan Mortensen headed England's first ever World Cup goal, Walter Winterbottom's team travelled from Rio de Janeiro to the mining town of Belo Horizonte to play the USA. Facing a side who had twice conceded six goals to Mexico in the qualifiers, England's stars were expected to win handsomely but after missing a host of chances and hitting the woodwork five times, they were beaten 1-0 in one of the tournament's greatest ever shocks. Another 1-0 defeat in their

Uruguay's Schiaffino equalises against Brazil

final match, this time against Spain, left England to ponder a first experience of the World Cup that had been a complete humiliation.

In a one-off experiment, the four group winners all played each other in a final pool, with the cup going to the country taking the most points. After scoring a total of 13 goals in their emphatic defeats of Sweden and Spain, this looked likely to be Brazil, especially as the hosts would only require a draw in their final match against neighbours Uruguay in the Maracana Stadium to become world champions.

A Brazilian triumph seemed even more certain when right-winger Friaca gave his side the lead just two minutes after the half-time break. Uruguay, though, responded with a series of attacks and were rewarded with an equaliser from Juan Alberto Schiaffino. Ten minutes from time the massed ranks of Brazilian fans in the record 199,854 crowd were stunned for a second time when Alcides Ghiggia fired in the winner for the visitors. Brazil had no answer and, after two decades, the World Cup returned to Uruguay.

1954, SWITZERLAND

England travelled to Switzerland with confidence at a low ebb after two shattering defeats at the hands of Hungary in the months before the World Cup. Their squad, though, was an experienced one, with an average age of 29 thanks in part to the presence of Stanley Matthews, still nipping down the wing at the age of 39.

The bizarre format of the tournament, the first to be televised, meant that the two seeded teams in each group would not play each other, only the other two supposedly weaker teams. England, then, avoided a potentially tricky fixture against Italy and instead opened their campaign against Belgium. The match was a thriller, the underdogs coming back from 3-1 down to force extra-time and, eventually, a 4-4 draw. Needing to beat the hosts to progress to the knockout stage, England won fairly comfortably thanks to goals by the Wolves duo, Jimmy Mullen and Dennis Wilshaw.

England's opponents in the quarter-finals were the holders

An injury to Puskas damaged Hungary's hopes in 1954

minutes from time German winger Helmut Rahn struck his second goal of the game to earn his country their first World Cup in dramatic fashion.

Uruguay, who had just trounced Scotland 7-0 in their final group match. Helped by some poor goalkeeping by Birmingham's Gil Merrick, the South Americans ran out 4-2 winners before going down by the same score to the brilliant Hungarians in the semi-finals. Their opponents in the final would be West Germany, who demolished Austria 6-1 in the other semi-final in Basel.

Having previously thrashed the Germans 8-3 in a group game, Hungary were strong favourites to triumph again in Berne and when they took a two-goal lead after just eight minutes the cup seemed destined for Budapest. Within another eight minutes, though, the Germans were level. Handicapped by an injury to their star player, inside-forward Ferenc Puskas, Hungary wilted and seven

1958, SWEDEN

England's preparations for the World Cup in Sweden were put into disarray in February 1958 by the Munich air crash, which claimed the lives of eight Manchester United players. Among the victims were three established England internationals – the great Duncan Edwards, striker Tommy Taylor and defender Roger Byrne – who would probably have featured in Walter Winterbottom's team had they survived.

Drawn in a tough group with eventual winners Brazil, Olympic champions the Soviet Union and the formidable Austrians, England's patched-up side got off to a reasonable start with a 2-2 draw against a physical Soviet outfit. A goalless draw against the talented Brazilians gave England a good chance of progressing, but a third stalemate against an already eliminated Austria meant they would have to meet the Soviets again in a play-off to decide who would go through to the quarter-finals. Resisting a fervent media campaign to start Manchester United's

A teenage Pele plays against Wales in 1958

20-year-old winger Bobby Charlton, Winterbottom saw his team go down to a 1-0 defeat and, frustratingly, return home from the competition before both Wales and Northern Ireland.

Both those teams, though, went out in the quarter-finals to end British interest in the tournament. Nothern Ireland were hammered 4-0 by France, while Wales were beaten by Brazil, 17-year-old striking sensation Pele grabbing the only goal. Pele then grabbed a hat-trick as Brazil crushed France 5-2 in one semi-final, while hosts Sweden saw off West Germany in the other.

In the final in Stockholm, Sweden took a surprise lead after just four minutes – but there was to be no shock result. Two goals by their centre-forward Vava put Brazil ahead before half-time, and the game was pretty much settled when Pele added a magnificent third 10 minutes after the break. Brazil's left-winger Mario Zagallo made it four with 13 minutes left and, although Sweden replied with a second goal, there was still time for Pele to round off a resounding victory for the South Americans with a majestic header.

1962, CHILE

With just two defeats in their previous 17 matches, an England team featuring the likes of goal poacher Jimmy

Brazil line up in traditional pose at the 1962 finals

Greaves, midfield playmaker Johnny Haynes and a young Bobby Moore in their line-up went into the 1962 World Cup in Chile in fine fettle. The confident mood, though, was soon shattered by a defeat to a Hungary side who

were not a patch on the 'Magical Magyars' of the 1950s. Written off by the press, England responded with an impressive 3-1 defeat of Argentina, Ron Flowers, Bobby Charlton and Greaves getting the goals for Walter Winterbottom's team. A dull 0-0 draw with Bulgaria then clinched England's place in the quarter-finals, where they had the misfortune to come up against the holders, Brazil.

Although missing Pele through injury, Brazil predictably proved too strong and ran out 3-1 winners, two of their goals coming from winger Garrincha, whose bandy-legged running style was the legacy of a childhood bout of polio. The other quarter-finals were won by Czechoslovakia, Yugoslavia and hosts Chile, who had earlier beaten Italy in one of the most violent games ever seen at the World Cup. Two Italian players were dismissed by the English referee Ken Aston, although the Chileans were equally to blame for some appalling scenes in a match dubbed 'The Battle of Santiago'.

The Chileans' underhand tactics were again in evidence in the semi-final, which they lost 4-2 to Brazil. Garrincha, who again netted twice, was kicked throughout, and when he finally retaliated was promptly sent off. It seemed that he would miss the final against Czechoslovakia, who beat Yugoslavia 3-1 in the other semi-final, until FIFA waived his suspension following a personal plea by the Brazilian President.

As in 1958 Brazil conceded the first goal in the final, but they were soon level through Pele's replacement Amarildo. The same player set up Zito for an easy header 20 minutes from time, before Vava ensured the cup would stay in Brazil by adding a third late on.

1966, ENGLAND

Hosting the World Cup for the first time, England went into the tournament as one of the favourites, the expectation of the nation intensified by manager Alf Ramsey's bold prediction that his side would win the competition.

Ramsey's confidence seemed misplaced after England opened their

Alan Ball's World Cup winner's medal from 1966

Bobby Moore shows off the World Cup at Wembley in 1966

shot which bounced down off the crossbar, the referee ruling that the ball had crossed the line after consulting his linesman. It was Hurst, too, who confirmed his team's triumph in the closing seconds with a rasping drive into the roof of the net, making him the first – and so far, only – player to score a hat-trick in a World Cup final.

1970, MEXICO

Often described as the best finals in the history of the competition, the 1970 tournament in Mexico provided a feast of attacking football – much of it served up by a wonderful Brazilian side featuring a host of legendary names including Pele, Rivelino and Jairzinho.

Brazil's match with holders England was the most keenly anticipated of the group stages, and lived up to expectations despite being played in blisteringly hot temperatures. England's goalkeeper Gordon Banks was in superb form, making a particularly memorable save from Pele's powerful header, but he was eventually beaten when Jairzinho rifled home what proved to be the winning goal. Victories over Romania and Czechoslovakia, though, saw England join Brazil in the quarter-finals.

campaign with a disappointing 0-0 draw with Uruguay, but a trademark Bobby Charlton thunderbolt against Mexico finally got the hosts going. A 2-0 victory over the Central Americans was followed by another comfortable win against France, in a match marred by an ugly tackle by Ramsey's midfield enforcer, Nobby Stiles.

In the quarter-finals, England struggled to break down an uncompromising and sometimes brutal Argentina, even after the first-half dismissal of their captain, Antonio Rattin. Eventually, though, Geoff Hurst headed the winner from a cross by his West Ham team-mate Martin Peters. After the final whistle Ramsey intervened to stop his players swapping shirts with their opponents, before describing the Argentinians as 'animals' in his post-match press conference.

England's semi-final with Portugal, who had recovered from 3-0 down to beat surprise package North Korea in the previous round, was a more attractive affair. Two goals from Bobby Charlton gave the home team a healthy cushion and, although Portugal star Eusebio scored from the spot late on, England marched on to their first World Cup final.

Their opponents at Wembley were West Germany, conquerors of the Soviet Union in the other semi-final. England got off to a poor start, conceding a sloppy goal to Helmut Haller after 12 minutes. Soon, though, Hurst equalised with a header from Bobby Moore's quickly taken free-kick and then, in the second half, went ahead when Peters slammed home from close range. With the last kick of the game, however, the Germans levelled with a scrappy goal by Wolfgang Weber.

'You've beaten them once... now go out and bloody beat them again!' Ramsey told his players before the start of extra-time. And that's precisely what they did. England restored their lead when Hurst struck a fierce

In a rerun of the 1966 final, England were paired with West Germany. Alf Ramsey's team seemed set for another

Carlos Alberto takes the Jules Rimet trophy for keeps

famous triumph when they swept into a 2-0 lead, but a mistake by goalkeeper Peter Bonetti, deputising for an unwell Banks, allowed Franz Beckenbauer to pull a goal back for the Germans. Ten minutes from time a back header from Uwe Seeler looped over Bonetti to level the scores, before prolific striker Gerd Muller completed a remarkable recovery with a close-range finish in extra-time.

The Germans' luck, though, ran out in the semi-final when they went down 4-3 to Italy in an extraordinary match which featured no fewer than five goals in extra-time. In the other semi-final, Brazil made light work of their neighbours Uruguay, winning 3-1 after another glittering display.

The final in Mexico City was a dazzling spectacle, providing a fitting end to a glorious tournament. Brazil took an early lead when Pele thumped in a header, but the Italians were on level terms before the break after Roberto Boninsegna was gifted a goal by the South Americans' erratic defence. There was no stopping Brazil in the second half, however, as Gerson rattled home a long-range shot, Jairzinho scored from close range and, finally, Pele stroked a pass into the path of his captain, Carlos Alberto, who blasted in a low piledriver from the edge of the box to round off his country's third World Cup victory in magnificent style.

1974, WEST GERMANY

The 1974 tournament is primarily remembered for some scintillating performances by a Dutch team appearing at their first post-war World Cup. Led by their imperious captain, the great Johan Cruyff, and adopting a fluid system of play dubbed 'Total Football', the Netherlands were simply sensational throughout.

The first round of matches, though, was most notable for the surprise elimination of Italy following a defeat by Poland, conquerors of England in the qualifiers. Another shock saw the hosts West Germany lose 1-0 to their East German neighbours, although both countries had already qualified for the second round.

For the first time, FIFA dispensed with the knockout format, instead opting for two groups of four teams from which the finalists would emerge. In the event, the last round of games provided semi-finals of sorts, the Netherlands beating a disappointing Brazil side 2-0 to top one group and West Germany defeating Poland thanks to a Gerd Muller goal on a waterlogged pitch in Frankfurt to head the other.

The final in Munich got off to an incredible start when a superb passing move by the Dutch straight from the kick-off ended with Cruyff being hacked

Johan Neeskens converts the Netherlands' penalty in the 1974 final

down in the penalty area. England's sole representative at the finals, referee Jack Taylor, pointed to the spot and Johan Neeskens converted the penalty – the fastest ever goal in a World Cup final. The Netherlands continued to dominate the game but their failure to extend their lead proved costly when the Germans equalised through Paul Breitner's penalty after 27 minutes. Worse was to follow for the Dutch when Muller put his side ahead just before half-time. The Netherlands found no way through after the break, and the tournament's outstanding team were denied the trophy their breathtaking football deserved.

1978, ARGENTINA

For a while it appeared that the 1978 tournament might not go ahead as planned in Argentina, following the imposition of a military dictatorship in the country. As worldwide protests against the generals' brutal regime gathered momentum there were demands for the finals to be played elsewhere, but FIFA refused to change the venue.

Whatever their political views, the Argentinian public supported their team with a passion rarely seen at previous tournaments, showering their heroes with ticker tape whenever they made their entrance. Despite losing their final group match to Italy, conquerors of England in the qualifiers, the home side easily progressed into the second round, which again was split into two pools of four. After

Mario Kempes scores in the World Cup final in 1978

picking up a win and a draw in their first two matches, the Argentinians needed to beat Peru by four goals in their last game to pip Brazil for a place in the final. To nobody's surprise, the Peruvians simply folded and were thrashed 6-0, strike partners Mario Kempes and Leopoldo Luque grabbing two goals each. Conspiracy theorists had a field day, suggesting that the Peruvians had either been bribed or that their goalkeeper, the Argentinian-born Ramon Quiroga, had given the hosts a helping hand.

The other final group was made up of four European teams: Austria, the Netherlands, Italy and West Germany. The key match was between the Netherlands and Italy, which the Dutch only needed to draw to reach the final. In the event, they won the game 2-1 despite trailing at half-time.

Roared on by a near-hysterical crowd in Buenos Aires, Argentina took the lead in the final through the prolific Kempes. A late equaliser by the Dutch sent the match into extra-time, but the hosts were not to be denied. Inspired by the midfield promptings of little Ossie Ardiles, they added further goals through Kempes and winger Daniel Bertoni to become world champions for the first time.

Trevor Francis helps outwit France in 1982

1982, SPAIN

After missing out on the two previous tournaments, England qualified for the first 24-team World Cup in unconvincing style. Once there, however, Ron Greenwood's team got off to a perfect start in their opening game against France when midfielder Bryan Robson drilled home after just 27 seconds – at the time, the second fastest goal in the competition's history. England went on to win the match 3-1, and after straightforward victories over Czechoslovakia and Kuwait, topped their group with something to spare.

A tough draw in the second stage saw England paired with old adversaries West Germany and hosts Spain. After a dull 0-0 with the Germans, England needed to beat the Spanish by two goals to reach the semi-finals but were held to another goalless draw. Frustratingly, two excellent chances were spurned by substitutes Kevin Keegan and Trevor Brooking, both making their first appearances of the finals after missing the earlier part of the tournament through injury.

In the first semi-final Italy, who had earlier sneaked through their first round group with three draws, beat Poland thanks to two goals by the tournament's top scorer, Paolo Rossi. Later that evening, an enthralling match between West Germany and France ended in a 3-3 draw after the French had led 3-1 in extra-time. For the first time ever at the World Cup a penalty shoot-out settled the outcome, the Germans emerging as the winners.

The first half of the final in Madrid was a tense affair, the best chance falling to the Italians when they were awarded a penalty. Left-back Antonio Cabrini, though, wasted the opportunity, sending his kick wide. In the end it mattered little, as Italy dominated after the break and scored three times through Rossi, Marco Tardelli and Alessandro Altobelli. Paul Breitner replied for the Germans, but far too late to prevent Italy claiming their third World Cup.

1986, MEXICO

Initially awarded to Colombia, the venue for the 1986 tournament was later switched for economic reasons to Mexico, who became the first nation to host the competition twice.

Maradona's 'Hand of God' goal against England   After a stress-free qualifying campaign,

England were expected to do well but they got off to a dreadful start, losing their opening match to Portugal and then being held by Morocco. Adding to manager Bobby Robson's woes, he also lost two of his key players, injured skipper Bryan Robson and midfielder Ray Wilkins, suspended after becoming the first England player to be sent off at the finals.

However, the new-look team Robson fielded in the must-win final group game against Poland performed much better, striker Gary Lineker scoring all three goals in a convincing 3-0 win. Another excellent display, and two more Lineker goals, saw off Paraguay in the last 16, setting up a quarter-final with Argentina.

The match in Mexico City hinged on two moments involving Diego Maradona, Argentina's captain and star player. Shortly after the break he flicked the ball into the net with his hand but, despite furious protests from England's players, the goal stood. Minutes later, Maradona dribbled past the entire England defence before planting the ball past goalkeeper Peter Shilton. Golden Boot winner Lineker replied with a late header, but it was not enough to save England.

Maradona scored another magical goal as Argentina breezed past Belgium and into the final. Their opponents were West Germany, conquerors of France in the other semi-final. The South Americans took a two-goal lead and appeared to be heading for a comfortable victory until the Germans scored twice in the final quarter hour, both goals coming from corners. There was still enough time left, though, for the brilliant Maradona to settle the game in Argentina's favour, his superb defence-splitting pass setting up midfielder Jorge Burruchaga for the winner.

1990, ITALY

The 1990 tournament in Italy provided some memorable moments but overall was a rather disappointing spectacle, plagued by overly-cautious football which resulted in the lowest goals-per-game average of any World Cup.

From an England perspective, though, the finals were the most exciting since Bobby Moore and co. triumphed in 1966. Nevertheless, Italia '90 started poorly for Bobby Robson's men with a draw against Ireland. Another draw, against a powerful Netherlands side, was more encouraging, midfielder Paul Gascoigne earning rave reviews for a dynamic performance. Qualification was

then achieved with a scrappy win over plucky minnows Egypt, defender Mark Wright scoring the only goal.

Under pressure from his senior players, Robson had switched to a sweeper system and he retained the formation for the last 16 meeting with Belgium. A tense game looked to be heading for penalties until Gascoigne's free-kick was superbly volleyed in by David Platt for the winner. 'Gazza', as he was now known to everybody, was again outstanding in a nerve-wracking quarter-final against surprise package Cameroon, which England won 3-2 in extra-time, with Gary Lineker firing in the second of two penalties to settle the match.

In the semi-final against West Germany in Turin England fell behind to a cruelly deflected free-kick, but hit back to equalise through Lineker. Extra-time brought no further goals, just a booking for a tearful Gazza – which meant he would miss the final should England get there. However, to the dismay of 30 million fans

Gazza before the tears in the 1990 semi-final against Germany

watching back home, both Stuart Pearce and Chris Waddle missed in the penalty shoot-out and the Germans went through.

Their opponents in Rome, Argentina, came through a semi-final shoot-out of their own, against Italy. An ugly, bad-tempered final, which saw two Argentinians dismissed, was also decided from the spot, West Germany's Andreas Brehme firing home late on to give his country a third world title.

1994, USA

For the first time in the history of the World Cup the 1994 tournament was held in a nation, the USA, where football is only a minor sport. Nevertheless, the American public responded enthusiastically, with the total attendance of 3.6 million being the highest ever at the finals so far.

The fans were rewarded with some exciting games in the opening round, and a number of shock results. Bulgaria beat Argentina, Saudi Arabia defeated Belgium while Jack Charlton's Ireland got the better of a highly-fancied Italy. All those teams went through to the second round, however, although Argentina did so without their captain Diego Maradona, who was sensationally banned from the rest of the tournament after failing a drugs test.

The South Americans were soon eliminated, losing a five-goal thriller to Romania in the last 16. Another east European team, Bulgaria, pulled off an even bigger surprise in the quarter-final when they came from behind to beat Germany. The Bulgarians' opponents in the semi-final were Italy, with Brazil and Sweden completing the final four. Both games were close, but neither of the underdogs survived: in Pasadena, the Swedes were undone by a late goal by Romario, while in New York, the Bulgarians succumbed to Italy's pony-tailed talisman Roberto Baggio, who claimed both goals in his side's 2-1 win.

The World Cup came to Chicago in 1994

In a repeat of the 1970 final, Italy and Brazil met to decide the destination of the trophy in Los Angeles. Despite the array of attacking talent on show, the game never really got going and it was no surprise that the tie had to be settled by penalties. Italy missed two and Brazil one before Baggio, the undoubted star of the tournament, blazed his kick high over the bar to gift the South Americans their fourth World Cup.

1998, FRANCE

The World Cup was revamped for the 1998 tournament in France, the most important innovations seeing the number of entrants expanding from 24 to 32 and the introduction of the 'golden goal' to settle knockout matches which went into extra-time.

Having missed out on the finals altogether four years earlier, England were determined to build on their good showing at Euro '96. Glenn Hoddle's side began with a comfortable victory over Tunisia in Marseille but then lost to Romania, falling to a last-minute winner by Dan Petrescu after 18-year-old striker Michael Owen had come off the bench to level the scores. Needing to beat

Zinedine Zidane after scoring in the 1998 final

Argentina's World Cup ended in the next round when they lost to the Netherlands, who in turn went out in a semi-final shoot-out to Brazil. The South Americans' opponents in the final were France, who came through their semi-final against surprise outfit Croatia thanks to two goals by defender Lilian Thuram.

Brazil's preparations for the final in Paris were thrown into turmoil when star striker Ronaldo suffered a convulsive fit shortly before kick-off. Although he played, Ronaldo understandably looked a shadow of his normal self and France won the match convincingly, two headers by their playmaker Zinedine Zidane settling the outcome before Emmanuel Petit added an extra gloss to the hosts' victory with a third goal in injury-time.

Colombia to advance, Darren Anderton and David Beckham came up with the goals to keep England in the tournament.

In the last 16 meeting with Argentina in St Etienne both sides netted from the spot in the early stages, before Owen put England ahead with a brilliant individual goal. However, the South Americans levelled the scores before half-time and then took the initiative when Beckham was sent off for a petulant kick at Diego Simeone who had fouled him. A man short, England hung on bravely through extra-time but lost out on penalties after misses by Paul Ince and David Batty.

2002, JAPAN AND SOUTH KOREA

The first World Cup to be held in Asia, the 2002 tournament in Japan and South Korea was attended by hordes of friendly supporters from the host nations. The local fans were repaid with consistently excellent displays by their own countries, who were among a number of less fancied teams to spring major surprises.

The main shock in the group stage was the elimination of holders France, after defeats by Senegal and Denmark. Portugal, too, fell by the wayside, following a 1-0 loss to South Korea. There was an upset, too, in England's

David Beckham converts a penalty against Argentina

group where Argentina failed to qualify, the key result being the South Americans' 1-0 defeat to Sven Goran Eriksson's men, England skipper David Beckham scoring from the penalty spot. The Three Lions had little difficulty in disposing of Denmark 3-0 in the last 16, thanks to Michael Owen, Emile Heskey, and an own goal.

In the quarter-final against Brazil, Owen gave his side the lead before Rivaldo equalised on the stroke of half-time. In the second half Ronaldinho floated a free-kick over David Seaman's head from fully 40 yards before being sent off. England, though, failed to make the extra man count and slipped out of the competition.

Both the semi-finals were decided by a single goal: Brazil accounting for Turkey and Germany finally seeing off South Korea, who had knocked out Italy and Spain in the previous rounds. In the first ever meeting between two titans of the World Cup, Ronaldo proved to be the difference between the teams, grabbing both goals as Brazil won 2-0 to claim a fifth World Cup title.

2006, GERMANY

An unwritten rule of the World Cup states that the winners virtually always come from the continent where the tournament is played. The 2006 finals in Germany took that rule a step further with all four semi-finalists hailing from Europe.

Among the European sides of whom great things were expected were Sven Goran Eriksson's England. Drawn in an easy-looking group and with a squad of players dubbed 'the golden generation', the Three Lions made painfully hard work of their opening fixtures, beating Paraguay by a single goal and taking more than 80 minutes to break the deadlock against Trinidad and Tobago before running out 2-0 winners. England then played much better against Sweden, but were held to a draw after the Scandinavians cancelled out a superb volley from Joe Cole and a Steven Gerrard header.

In the last 16, England were unconvincing once more against Ecuador, surviving a number of scares before skipper David Beckham's free-kick proved decisive. With Michael Owen sidelined by injury, Eriksson adopted a cautious strategy against Portugal in the quarter-final, employing Wayne Rooney as a lone striker. The game turned out to be a cagey affair, the key moment coming when Rooney was sent off for stamping on Ricardo Carvalho. England hung on grimly through extra-time before the match was settled by penalties. The old shoot-out hoodoo struck again as Frank Lampard, Gerrard and Jamie Carragher all missed.

Wayne Rooney sees red in the 2006 quarter-final

The Portuguese, though, were not so fortunate in the semi-final against France, going out to a Zinedine Zidane spot-kick. The other semi-final between Italy and Germany was set to go to penalties until the hosts were undone by two goals at the end of extra-time.

The final in Berlin got off to a spectacular start when France were awarded a controversial penalty after just seven minutes. Zidane, cool as ever, chipped his shot in off the crossbar, but Italy levelled soon afterwards through Marco Materazzi's firm header. Both sides missed chances to win the match before Zidane was sent off in extra-time for head-butting Materazzi in the chest. Italy failed to take advantage of their numerical superiority and, as in 1994, the final was decided by the lottery of penalties. The fall guy on this occasion was France's David Trezeguet, whose miss allowed Fabio Grosso the chance to clinch the trophy. Showing no sign of nerves, the left-back swept the ball high into the corner of the net and Italy were world champions for a fourth time.

2010, SOUTH AFRICA

The first World Cup to be played in Africa generated huge anticipation and support across the continent and, for England, the familiar feeling of expectation after an impressive qualifying campaign. The Three Lions may have had a new manager in Fabio Capello, but it was the same old story as the fading embers of the golden generation flattered to deceive.

A draw with the USA best remembered for a howler by goalkeeper Rob Green and a forgettable goalless stalemate against Algeria meant England needed to beat Slovenia to advance to the last 16, which they did thanks to Jermain Defoe's strike.

That was as far as they would go, though, as a rampant Germany put them to the sword. England were left to rue what might have been when Frank Lampard's shot clearly bounced over the line but was not awarded as a goal. That would have made the score 2-2 yet, from there, they capitulated to a 4-1 defeat.

Germany put four more past an Argentina side managed by Diego Maradona to advance to the semi-finals where they were edged out 1-0 by Spain, a repeat of the scoreline from the Euro 2008 final. It was the third 1-0 win for the miserly Spanish, and their fifth clean sheet of the tournament.

Two other leading European nations did not even reach the knockout phase. Defending champions Italy finished bottom of their group, drawing with Paraguay and New Zealand, then losing to Slovakia. Their opponents in the 2006 final, France, departed alongside South Africa from a group topped by Uruguay.

The host nation's elimination meant the whole continent threw their support behind Ghana, the one African country to qualify for the last 16. They had reason to cheer when Asamoah Gyan scored the winner in extra-time against the USA, but the striker could not repeat his match-winning heroics in the quarter-final, missing a penalty with the very last kick of the game. He was not the main villain of the piece, however: that

role fell to Uruguay's Luis Suarez who, in the incident that led to the penalty, deliberately handled the ball on the line to prevent a Ghanaian goal. With the match ending 1-1, Uruguay won the ensuing shoot-out, sending all of Africa into mourning.

The South Americans' opponents in the semi-final were the Netherlands, who had stunned Brazil in the last eight, a Wesley Sneijder brace overturning a one-goal deficit. And Sneijder was on target once again as the Dutch ended Uruguay's hopes with a 3-2 win in the last four.

That result meant there would be a new name on

Andres Iniesta fires home the winning goal in the 2010 final

the trophy in the decider in Johannesburg. The final, refereed by Howard Webb, was a hot-headed encounter, with the Englishman booking 13 players including the dismissal of Dutchman Johnny Heitinga for two yellow cards. With the Spanish defence proving impregnable once again, Andres Iniesta settled the tie with the only goal deep into extra-time. Another 1-0 win for Spain, the eighth winners of the World Cup.

WORLD CUP RECORDS

TEAM RECORDS

• The most successful country in the history of the World Cup are Brazil, who have won the competition a record five times – in 1958, 1962, 1970, 1994 and 2002.

• **Italy are Europe's leading nation with four wins, closely followed by three-time winners Germany. South American neighbours Argentina and Uruguay have both won the competition twice, the Uruguayans emerging victorious when the pair met in the first ever World Cup final in Montevideo in 1930. The only other countries to claim the trophy are England (1966), France (1998) and current holders Spain (2010).**

• Including both Japan and South Korea, who were joint hosts for the 2002 edition, the World Cup has been staged in 16 different countries.

• **The first nation to stage the tournament twice**

Cafu gets his hands on the World Cup – after someone got their hands on his shirt!

were Mexico (in 1970 and 1986), while Italy (1934 and 1990), France (1938 and 1998) and Germany (1974 and 2006) have also played the role of hosts on two occasions. Brazil, hosts for the first time in 1950, will join this particular club once the 2014 tournament kicks off.

• Brazil are the only country to have played at all 19 tournaments, and will stretch their record to 20 in 2014. Along with Germany, the South Americans have played in a record seven finals. Germany have played in the most games (99) but Brazil are out in front when it comes to total wins (67) and total goals scored (210), including a few memorable ones from the likes of Pele, Socrates and Ronaldo.

• **Hungary hold the record for the most goals scored in a single tournament, banging in 27 in just five games at the 1954 finals in Switzerland. Even this impressive tally, though, was not quite enough for the 'Magical Magyars' to lift the trophy as they lost 3-2 in the final against West Germany, a team they had annihilated 8-3 earlier in the tournament.**

• Hungary also hold the record for the biggest ever victory at the finals, demolishing El Salvador 10-1 at the 1982 tournament in Spain. That, though, was a reasonably close encounter compared to the biggest win in qualifying, Australia's 31-0 massacre of American Samoa in 2001, a game in which Aussie striker Archie Thompson smashed in a record 13 goals.

• **A record five countries were unbeaten at the 2006 finals in Germany: winners Italy, runners-up France plus Argentina, England and Switzerland, who were all defeated on penalties in the knockout rounds.**

INDIVIDUAL RECORDS

• The legendary Pele is the only player in World Cup history to have been presented with three winner's medals. The Brazilian striker enjoyed his first success as a 17-year-old in 1958 when he scored twice in a 5-2 rout of hosts Sweden in the final, and was a winner again four years later in Chile despite hobbling out of the tournament with a torn leg muscle in the second match. He then made it a hat-trick in 1970, setting a brilliant Brazil side on the road to a convincing 4-1 victory against Italy in the final with a superb header.

• The leading overall scorer in the World Cup is another famous Brazilian, Ronaldo, who notched 15 goals in total at three tournaments between 1998 and 2006, including both goals in his side's 2-0 defeat of Germany in the 2002 final. The individual tournament scoring record is held by French striker Just Fontaine, who scored 13 goals at the 1958 finals in Sweden.

• England's Geoff Hurst is the only player to score a hat-trick in a World Cup final, finding the net three times against West Germany at Wembley in 1966. His second goal, which gave England a decisive 3-2 lead in extra-time, was the most controversial in World Cup history and German fans still maintain that his shot bounced on the line after striking the crossbar, rather than over it. Naturally, England fans tend to agree with the eagle-eyed Russian linesman who awarded the goal.

• Just two players have appeared at a record five World Cups: German midfield general Lothar Matthaus (1982-98) and Mexican goalkeeper Antonio Carbajal (1950-66). Matthaus, though, holds the record for games played in the finals, making 25 appearances for his country.

• The youngest player to appear at the finals is Norman Whiteside, who was just 17 and 41 days when he made his World Cup debut for Northern Ireland against Yugoslavia at the 1982 tournament in Spain. The competition's oldest player, meanwhile, is Cameroon's Roger Milla, who was aged 42 and 39 days when he played against Russia in 1994. It was hardly a day to remember for the veteran striker, though, as Russia won 6-1 with a record five goals coming from the boot of Oleg Salenko.

• England's Peter Shilton (1982-90) and France's Fabien Barthez (1998-2006) jointly hold the record for most clean sheets at the finals, with 10 each. Italy's Walter Zenga, though, holds the record for the most consecutive clean sheets, keeping the ball out of his net for a staggering 517 minutes at the 1990 tournament.

• The fastest goal in World Cup history was scored by Hakan Sukur, who struck for Turkey after just 11 seconds in the third place play-off against hosts South Korea in 2002. Hungary's Laszlo Kiss scored the fastest hat-trick, finding the net three times in eight minutes after coming on as a sub against El Salvador in 1982.

He may have been 42, but Roger Milla could celebrate with the best of them

No wonder Italy were excited in 2006 – they had finally won a penalty shoot-out

MISCELLANEOUS RECORDS

• Living up to their reputation for ruthless efficiency, Germany are the most successful side in World Cup shoot-outs, winning all four of their penalty duels including one in 1990 when they beat England in the semi-finals before going on to lift the trophy after a scrappy 1-0 victory over Argentina in the final.

• As most England fans know, the Three Lions have a dreadful record in World Cup shoot-outs, losing all three they have been involved in: against Germany in 1990, Argentina in 1998, and Portugal in 2006. The only other country to lose three shoot-outs are Italy, although they finally managed to win one when they defeated France on penalties in the 2006 final.

• The most unfortunate country in World Cup history are Scotland, who have made eight appearances at the finals without once advancing to the knockout stages. The Scots, though, were desperately unfortunate to be eliminated on goal difference in 1974, 1978 and 1982. Mexico, meanwhile,

have appeared at a record 14 finals without once advancing beyond the quarter-final stage.

• The most-played match at the World Cup is between Brazil and Sweden, the two sides having met seven times between 1938 and 1994. Brazil won five of the games, including a 5-2 victory in the 1958 final, while the other two encounters were drawn.

• Argentina have the worst disciplinary record at the finals, having a record 10 players sent off and 95 cautioned (another record) in just 69 games. The earliest red card, meanwhile, was shown to Uruguay hatchetman Jose Batista, who was given his marching orders after just 56 seconds against Scotland in 1986.

• The only player to score for both teams in a World Cup match is the Netherlands' Ernie Brandts, who found the net at both ends in a 2-1 defeat of Italy in 1978.

• Discounting goals scored in shoot-outs, three players have notched a record four penalties at the World Cup: Portugal's Eusebio in 1966, the Netherlands' Rob Rensenbrick in 1978 and Gabriel Batistuta with two for Argentina at both the 1994 and 1998 tournaments.

• The highest scoring match at the finals saw Austria beat hosts Switzerland 7-5 in 1954. The Austrians recovered from 3-0 down to win the match, a feat matched by Portugal when they beat North Korea 5-3 in the quarter-final at Goodison Park in 1966.

• **The record attendance for a World Cup match is 199,854 at the 1950 final between Brazil and Uruguay at the Maracana Stadium in Rio de Janeiro. The lowest attendance stands at just 300 for the 1930 clash between Peru and Romania in Montevideo.**

• Bora Milutinovic coached a record five countries at the World Cup finals, starting out with Mexico in 1986. The much-travelled Yugoslav then moved on to Costa Rica (1990), USA (1994), Nigeria (1998) and, finally, China (2002). Carlos Alberto Parreira, meanwhile, has coached four different countries at a record six finals: Kuwait (1982), Saudi Arabia (1990 and 1998), Brazil (1994 and 2006) and South Africa (2010).

• **The only coach to win the trophy twice is Vittorio Pozzo, with Italy in 1934 and 1938. Just two men have won the competition as both a player and a coach: Brazil's Mario Zagallo (in 1958, 1962 and 1970) and Germany's Franz Beckenbauer (in 1974 and 1990).**

• Ghana's Asamoah Gyan is the only player to miss two penalties at the finals, fluffing his lines against the Czech Republic in 2006 and against Uruguay four years later.

ENGLAND RECORDS

• Goalkeeper Peter Shilton holds the record for the most England appearances at the World Cup finals, playing in 17 matches between 1982 and 1990. Shilton is also the oldest England player to feature at the tournament, making his last appearance aged 40 and 295 days against hosts Italy in the play-off for third place in 1990.

• **With 10 goals to his name Gary Lineker is England's record scorer at the World Cup. Lineker struck six times at the 1986 tournament – itself**

Gary Lineker scored a record 10 World Cup goals for England

a record by an England player – to win the Golden Boot, and then added four more goals at Italia '90 to help his country reach the semi-finals. Along with Geoff Hurst, Lineker is also one of just two England players to score a hat-trick at the finals, grabbing all three of his team's goals in a 3-0 win against Poland in 1986.

• The only England player to be selected for four World Cups is Bobby Charlton, although he failed to make an appearance at his first tournament in Sweden in 1958. If Ashley Cole is selected for Brazil 2014, he will become the second player to achieve this. David Beckham is the only England player to have scored at three finals, netting against Colombia (1998), Argentina (2002) and Ecuador (2006).

David Beckham is the only England player to have scored at three World Cups

• **England scored a record 11 goals at the 1966 finals, and also enjoyed a record streak of five consecutive wins at the tournament on their way to lifting the Jules Rimet trophy. A sixth consecutive win followed with victory over Romania in England's first match of the 1970 finals in Mexico.**

• Manchester United midfielder Bryan Robson scored the fastest ever England goal – and the third fastest in World Cup history – when he struck after just 27 seconds against France in 1982. England went on to win the match 3-1.

• **The youngest England player to appear at the World Cup is Michael Owen, who was aged 18 and 183 days when he came on as a sub against Tunisia in 1998. Seven days later Owen became England's youngest ever scorer at the finals when he fired home in a 2-1 defeat by Romania.**

• England used a record 19 players at the 1970, 1986,

1990 and 2010 tournaments. At the other end of the scale, in an era when substitutes were not permitted, England used just 12 players at the 1962 finals.

• **Three players have captained England at a record 10 World Cup matches: Billy Wright (1950-58), Bobby Moore (1966-70) and David Beckham (2002-06).**

• Just three England players have been sent off at the World Cup: Ray Wilkins (for throwing the ball at the referee against Morocco in 1986); David Beckham (for retaliating after being fouled against Argentina in 1998); and Wayne Rooney (for stamping on an opponent against Portugal in 2006).

• **England have only managed to score four goals in a World Cup match on two occasions, in a 4-4 draw against Belgium in 1954 and in the famous 4-2 win against West Germany in the 1966 final at Wembley.**

Match-by-Match Scorechart

SECOND ROUND

MATCH 1
Sat Jun 28 (5.00pm) — Belo Horizonte

1st Group A — 2nd Group B

MATCH 2
Sat Jun 28 (9.00pm) — Rio de Janeiro

1st Group C — 2nd Group D

MATCH 3
Sun Jun 29 (5.00pm) — Fortaleza

1st Group B — 2nd Group A

MATCH 4
Sun Jun 29 (9.00pm) — Recife

1st Group D — 2nd Group C

MATCH 5
Mon Jun 30 (5.00pm) — Brasilia

1st Group E — 2nd Group F

MATCH 6
Mon Jun 30 (9.00pm) — Porto Alegre

1st Group G — 2nd Group H

MATCH 7
Tue Jul 1 (5.00pm) — Sao Paulo

1st Group F — 2nd Group E

MATCH 8
Tue Jul 1 (9.00pm) — Salvador

1st Group H — 2nd Group G

QUARTER-FINALS

QF 1
Fri Jul 4 (5.00pm) — Rio de Janeiro

Winner Match 5 — Winner Match 6

QF 2
Fri Jul 4 (9.00pm) — Fortaleza

Winner Match 1 — Winner Match 2

QF 3
Sat Jul 5 (5.00pm) — Brasilia

Winner Match 7 — Winner Match 8

QF 4
Sat Jul 5 (9.00pm) — Salvador

Winner Match 3 — Winner Match 4

All kick-offs are in British Summer Time